John Deere Farm Toys:

Identification Guide, Value Guide, And Inventory List

Second Edition

Bill Vossler

Bill Vossler Books

Disclaimer:
This book is a *guide.* No responsibility can revert to the author for any transaction into which collectors may enter using this book.

Cover Photos: Ertl/Racing Champions

Design: Bill Vossler

ISBN 0-9708041-2-1

Printed in the United States of America
by Park Press,
Waite Park, Minnesota

Published by
Bill Vossler Books
P.O. Box 372
Rockville, Minnesota 56369

Contents

How To Grade Farm Toys

Grading farm toys is tricky business, and in fact, many collectors would rather ignore grading, and simply come to an agreement on how much they want to pay for a toy ("You couldn't come down $5 on that, could you?) or how much they want to sell it for, rather than figure out what grade it might fall into, and arrive at a price from there. However, the reality is that every time a collector buys or sells a toy, *they are actually grading it.* Otherwise, all toys would be priced the same. During each transaction collectors ask, "Is this toy worth that much?" And if it is--or isn't--they are making that decision based heavily on the condition of the toy, whether the condition of that toy is named, or not.

For many years, that has been perfectly acceptable. But nowadays with purchasing toys through the mail, the advent of the internet, telephone bidding at auctions--any situation where the collector cannot actually see or handle the toy--another method is needed to determine how much to pay for a toy.

Every other major hobby has an accepted grading scale, although, as in coin collecting, not everyone agrees on how efficient or useful the scale is. However, coins deal in minutiae--how much of the torch is worn off? How legible is the date? Do facial high points show clearly? Whereas farm toys deal in miniatures, and at least down to the 1/32 scale, most markers that help determine toy condition are relatively easy to determine--any major paint scrapes? Any parts missing? Any major blemishes?

Perhaps it is time for the farm toy hobby to start thinking about a single, unified scale to determine the condition of a farm toy; the following information, courtesy of Kurt Aumann of Aumann Auctions, Inc. of Nokomis, Illinois, is not only a useful scale, but also a strong starting point for such a debate:

Sometimes the condition of a farm toy is pretty obvious, like with this battered old (but rare) John Deere A from the 1940s. The paint from the body is missing and peeling, the rubber tires are worn, and in general, the toy is in poor condition.

Then there are toys like this one, where some paint is obvious chipped off in different spots--a toy that was played with--but other spots, like around the engine, the paint looks pretty good. How would you grade this toy if you were selling or buying?

Notes on Toy Grading

As Kurt says, "When grading a toy, it is a difficult task to convey to another person the condition the toy is in. These ratings and descriptions are only a guide. Personal inspection is recommended when possible or after inspection, asking a series of questions to get information you would like to know about the toy.

"Many toys are old, and that needs to be taken into consideration. The "perfect" toy may be a product of legend, because it is always possible to find a flaw on any toy. Please note that rarity and age of toy are taken into consideration when grading. Toys are graded in comparison to other examples of the same toy. Newer toys are graded more critically than cast iron toys for instance, which are much older.

Toy Grading Scale

Mint: A mint toy can be expected to look like it did when it left the factory. No paint chips, never played with or taken apart. Factory flaws--paint run, crooked decal--that don't affect the toy's value will still allow the toy to be considered mint if the toy left the factory in that condition.

Near Mint (95% to 99%) – A toy in this condition has had minor wear, if any. The toy appears mint, but on close inspection some minor flaws will appear. One or several very small blemishes, scratches or very small chips may appear in the paint. The toy has probably not been played with,

but is not perfect. 95% to 99% of the original paint exists on the tractor.

90% to 94% - The toy has had gentle play. It is in good condition, but has either more paint flaws or more severe paint flaws than a near mint toy. It is still a very respectable original toy in need of no restoration work of any sort. 90% to 94% of the original paint exists on the tractor.

80% to 89% - A toy in this range has been played with and show wears in the form of rubs, scratches, parts wear and paint chips. Everything on the toy is original and the toy has 80% to 90% of the original paint left on the toy.

70% to 79% - A toy has been played with and shows considerable wear. Some parts may fit very loosely. Everything on the toy is still original and it retains 70% to 79% of its original paint.

50% to 69% - A toy in this range has considerable wear on both paint and parts. Minor parts may be missing (ex. steering wheel) and the toy may have minor damage. The toy is a candidate to some as a restoration project.

Below 50%. Toys that rate below 50% are con-
sidered rebuilder toys and are candidates for restoration. These toys have major paint loss and could have parts missing.

Collectors with questions can contact Kurt Aumann at 217-563-2523. Some collectors might question a grading system, because it's new, or wondering how to learn if a toy is, say 65%. The answer is simple: practice. Collectors need to work at it until figuring out what grade a toy is becomes second nature.

It's easy to figure out when a toy is in superb condition--as with this John Deere unit still behind its original cellophane. Even a cursory check will determine that this toy is in the best of condition, and will therefore has considerably more value.

A rare toy like this John Deere carry-scraper, or dirt scraper, is greatly affected by the condition that is placed on it when a collector wants to buy or sell. Collectors who know how to grade can save--or make--themselves hundreds of dollars.

Using This Price Guide

A price guide is only as good as the person who uses it--"guide" being the operative word. A price guide should never be used as a club--i.e., "This guide says my Vindex D is worth $1500 in excellent, and you're offering me $1400!" In the end, the guide is only a starting point; it will offer a general estimate of what your Vindex D is worth.

There are many reasons why prices can't be exact: condition of the toy, desire to buy or sell, the market (although JD collectors can be heartened that their toys are the most popular--half of all farm toy collectors--and also because JD toys hold and increase their value, in general, more than other farm toys.

Farm toy prices are either stagnant or down, except for Precision Series toys and many custom-made toys. Most others stayed the same or dropped $5 to $20 a toy, which doesn't really matter to most collectors.

Reading Photo References

☐ A, 1947, Lincoln, SCA, Driver, Closed Flywheel, Firestone Tires, NF, Canadian, 1504, Excellent-NIB $300-700
Notes:

Above is an actual and typical reference from ***John Deere Farm Toys.*** First comes a check-box for inventory, (☐) followed by the John Deere make ("A"), the year it was *first* manufactured, (1947), the company that made it, (Lincoln, or "Lincoln Specialties of Canada"--see the "Manufacturers' Abbreviations" section); followed by pertinent information about the toy (SCA, for "sand-cast aluminum"), (Closed Flywheel, Firestone Tires, NF--short for "narrow front"--see the general "Abbreviations" section, and "Canadian".) Then comes the "Stock Number" (1504, made-up for this example only), followed by the value of the toy. This can be in Excellent condition ("Excellent $400"), or NIB (new-in-box) or NIP (new-in-package, for smaller scales of toys.) For example, "NIB $225", or "NIP $4". Or a range, like for the Lincoln A: "$300-700", which means "from $300 in Excellent to $700 NIB." Finally, some toy prices are "NA", or "not available", for several reasons.

All this information on each toy is followed either by a listing of another and very similar toy, but with different information--special edition, demonstrator, "Land of Lincoln Show", and so on.

After that, in most cases, there is space for notes about your own toys.

The sizes of the toys are indicated in boxes at the top and bottom of each page, and are generally in order, after the most common scale of 1/16, throughout the book, that is, all pages of 1/16 scale toys in alphabetic and then numerical order (A, AR, B, etc., 3010, 3020, and so on). The book also is divided into sections by general use of the machine on the farm: tractors, implements & machinery, industrials & crawlers, sets, pedals, and the like. In addition, several hundred toys are listed in the back of the book, without photos, either because they closely duplicated toys that are in the photo section, because photos were not available, or because they were custom-made, and there are hundreds--perhaps over a thousand people customizing (some very superbly) John Deere toys, and it was impossible to not only stay abreast of all of them--a moving target--but also to get photos of them. So if you don't find the toy you're looking for in the photo section, check the toy list at the back of the book; they are listed similarly to the Lincoln A listed for example above.

John Deere Farm Tractors

Identification Guide, Value Guide, And Inventory List

Manufacturer Abbreviations

ATT is A T & T Collectables, Anton Kupka
AMT, American Model Toys
Arcor is Auburn Rubber Co.
Bosso, Uruguay
Brown is Brown_ s Models, England
Buhler, larry buhler canada
Burt is Burt Industries
CC is Custom Cast
EFS, Elmira Farm Service, Canada
FC or FLCL Florida Classic
Gunning is Tom Gunning
Jergenson is Earl Jergenson
K & G is K&G Sand Casting
Keith is Steve Keith
Kruse is Marvin Kruse
Lincoln is Lincoln Specialties
L&J is L&J Replicas
LW is Lee Wayne Co.
N. B. & K. is N. B.& K. Enterprises
OTC is Old Time Collectibles
Parker is Dennis Parker
PTW is Pioneer Tractor Works
PC is Pioneer Collectibles
PPC is Precision Pewter Cast
Price is Price Products--Prio
Pro is Pro-tractor Replicas
Rawcliff is Rawcliff Corp.
Riecke is Riecke Farm Models
Rogers is Ken Rogers Company
Stoller is Harlan E. Stoller
Sharp is David Sharp
Stephan is Stephan Manufacturing
Trumm is Eldon Trumm
Woodlands is Woodlands Scenics
Yoder is Yoder's Custom Service
Deyzel is Jonnie Deyzel
S&T is Steam & Truck
Nolt is Nolt Enterprises, Inc.
Burt is Burt Industries
Haag is Terry Haag
Baird is Charles Baird
Kaufman is John Kaufman
Matsen is Dale Matsen
Hoover is Hoover Mfg Co.
Krominga is Delwin Krominga of Iowa
Murphy is Jos. F. Murphy, Inc.
Van Hove is Lyle Van Hove

Other Abbreviations

2WD or 4WD mean two- or four-wheel drive
3 pt or 3 point is 3-point hitch
CA is cast aluminum, CZ is cast zinc
FWA is front wheel assist
MFWD is mechanical front-wheel drive
NF or N/F is narrow front-end
NIB is new in box, NIP is new in package
PL is plastic
PS is pressed steel
PTO is power take-off
ROPS is roll-over protection system
SCA is sand-cast aluminum
WF or WFE is wide front end

☐ **A, 1940, Arcade, Cast Iron, Nickeled Man, Rubber Wheels, NF, Excellent-NIB $700-2800**
Notes:

☐ **A, 1945, Ertl, CA, NF, Molded-in Driver, Open Flywheel, Aluminum Wheels, Very Rare, Rarely Found In Good Shape, Excellent, $1500**
Notes:

☐ **A, 1946, Ertl, CA, NF, Driver, Open Flywheel, Headlights, On Rubber, Arcade Front Wheels, Excellent-NIB $250-750**
Notes:

☐ **A, 1947, Ertl, CA, Closed Flywheel, Driver, NF, Smooth Front Tires, Excellent-NIB $160-600**
Notes:

☐ **A, 1947, Lincoln, SCA, Driver, Closed Flywheel, Firestone Tires, NF, Canadian, Excellent-NIB $300-700**
Notes:

☐ **A, 1981, ScaMo, SCA, 7th In JLE Collector Series I, Spoke Wheels, 3000 Made, Excellent-NIB $30-40**
☐ **ALSO SAME, Except Brass, Excellent-NIB $75-85**
Notes:

☐ **A, 1984, Ertl, Die, Rubber Tires, Shelf Model, 539DO, Excellent-NIB $10-18**
Notes:

☐ **A, 1984, Ertl, Die, "50th Anniversary 1934-1984," Spoke Wheels, Limited Edition, 538DO, Excellent-NIB $30-40**
Notes:

☐ **A, 1985, Ertl, Die, "40th Anniversary Of Ertl," On Rubber, Driver, 539DO, Excellent-NIB $10-18**
☐ **ALSO SAME, Except Gold, Rare (SEE COLOR PLATES.) NA**
☐ **1986, Limited Edition, 557DA, Excellent-NIB $32-45**
Notes:

☐ **A, 1987, ScaMo, Repro Of First Ertl Tractor, Driver, Aluminum Tires, "3rd Generation" Inside Rear Tires, Excellent-NIB $25-35**
Notes:

☐ **A, 1989, ScaMo, Die, On Rubber, Open Flywheel, Beckman Endowment, Excellent-NIB $30-40**
Notes:

☐ **A, 1990, Ertl, Die, Unstyled, Precision Classics, Highly Detailed, 560CO, Excellent-NIB $125-235**
☐ **ALSO SAME, Except, 1993, "JD Parts Expo", Or "Nashville", Or "Louisville", 560CA, Exc-NIB $150-265**
Notes:

□ A, 1990, ScaMo, Die, Wyoming Centennial, 5000 Made, WYC19-910, Excellent-NIB $30-45
Notes:

□ A, 1991, Riecke, NF, Custom, Excellent $300
Notes:

□ A, 1991, Ertl, Die, With Cultivator, 2nd Precision Classic Series, 5633CO, Excellent-NIB $300-475
Notes:

□ A, 1992, ScaMo, Die, "1992 World Ag Expo," On Steel, With Fenders, FB-1594, Excellent-NIB $30-40
Notes:

□ A, 1995, ScaMo, Die, With Farmhand Hay Loader, NIB $220
Notes:

□ A, 1996, Ertl, Die, NF, Foxfire Series, With Red Mccune Figure, 5702DO, NIB $30
Notes:

☐ A, 1998, Ertl, Die, WWKI, "We Care," 1st In Series, Spoke Wheels, On Rubber, Serial Numbered, 5000 Made, NIB $40
Notes:

☐ A, 1998, Weber, Acrylic, See-Through, Interior Workings Visible, Extremely Rare, NA
Notes:

☐ A, 1998, Ertl, Die, With Umbrella, "South Dakota FFA," Limited Edition, 500 Made, 29049T, NIB $50
☐ ALSO SAME, Except No Spoke Rear Wheels, "Michigan FFA," Limited Edition, 2500 Made, NIB $60
Notes:

☐ A, 2001, SpecCast, Resin, On Sculptured Base, JDM 167, NIB $65
Notes:

☐ Different Toy companies and shows deal with logos in different ways; in this case, the 1991 Elmira Toy Celebration logo is a decal on top of the hood.
Notes:

☐ A, 2002, Ertl, Die, Shelf Model, 15071, NIB $22
Notes:

☐ **AO, 1992, Protractor, Spin, On Steel Or Rubber, NIB $250**
Notes:

☐ **AR, 1980s, ATT, Unstyled On Rubber Tires, Crude, NIB $35**
Notes:

☐ **AR, 1989, AMTI, SCA, Standard, Excellent-NIB $30-35**
Notes:

☐ **AR, 1994, Stephan, Custom, NIB $265**
Notes:

☐ **AR, 1994, ScaMo, Die, Farm Progress Days, FB-2353, Excellent-NIB $32-45**
Notes:

☐ **AR, 1998, Ertl, Die, Foxfire, 19th In Series, “Elery Parks And Dog Smokey” Figure, 5093DO, NIB $38**
Notes:

☐ **AR, 2000, Ertl, Die, NIB $35**
Notes:

☐ **AR, 1999, Ertl, Die, 1999 "1999 C.I.F.E.S" (Canadian International Farm Equipment Show), 500 Made, Serial Numbered, 5093DO, NIB $60**
Notes:

☐ **AW, 2000, Ertl, Die, With Umbrella, Collector Edition, 15070, NIB $42**
Notes:

☐ **B, 1950, Ertl, SCA, No Driver, NF, Highpost B, (Often Called "Highpost A"), Excellent-NIB $250-650**
☐ **ALSO SAME, Except Red With Yellow Wheels, Dime Store Edition, Scarce, Excellent $750**
Notes:

☐ **B, 1986, Riecke, Custom, Steel Wheels Or Rubber Tires, Excellent $225**
Notes:

☐ **B, 1988, NB & K, SC, "2nd Annual Florida Show Tractor," 1227 Made, Serial Numbered, Excellent-NIB $80-100**
Notes:

☐ **B, 1994, ScaMo, Die, Farm Progress Days, FB-2352, NIB $75**
Notes:

☐ **B, 1996, Ertl, Die, 1935 Model B 4-Bolt Tractor (In Front Of Pedestal), Collector Series, 5822DA, NIB $30**
Notes:

☐ **B, 1996, Ertl, Die, 1937 Model B 8-Bolt Tractor, (8 Bolts In Pedestal Above Front Wheels), 5904DO, NIB $25**
Notes:

☐ **B, 1997, Ertl, Die, Iowa FFA Foundation, FFA Umbrella, 4833TA, NIB $70**
Notes:

☐ **B, 1997, Ertl, Die, Precision Classic #12, 5107CO, NIB $150**
Notes:

☐ **B, 1997, Ertl, W/Wagon & Corn, Foxfire, Driver, TBE5341, NIB $40**
Notes:

□ B, 2001, Danbury Mint, Cold-Cast Porcelain, Clock In Rear Wheel, NIB $65
Notes:

□ B, 2002, Ertl, Die, 1936 Model With Firestone Tires, 7,500 Made, NIB $68
Notes:

□ BN, 2000, Ertl, Die, TBE5902, NIB $25
Notes:

□ BO, 2000, SpecCast, Die, JDM 151, NIB $35
□ ALSO SAME, Rubber Tires, Metal Rims, JDM117, NIB $35
Notes:

□ BR, 1986, Riecke, Custom, On Steel Or Rubber, Excellent $225
Notes:

□ BR, 1988, Ertl, Die, Shelf 5586DO, Excell-NIB $17-25
□ ALSO, SAME, Except Dated Insert, Collector Model, 48 Per Dealer, 5586DA, Excellent-NIB $20-30
□ ALSO, SAME, Except Steel Wheels, 1988 Special Edition, 5586EO, Excellent-NIB $20-30

☐ **BR, 1997, Ertl, Die, 5761DO, NIB $25**
Notes:

☐ **BW, 1996, Ertl, Die, BW-40, "1996 2-Cylinder Club," 5000 Made, 5824TA, NIB $165**
Notes:

☐ **BW, 2002, Ertl/RC, Die, Wide Front, TBE15348, NIB $30**
Notes:

☐ **C, 1993, Ertl, Die, Special Edition, "Two Cylinder Club Center Grand Opening," 5700TA, Exc-NIB $40-47**
☐ **ALSO SAME But "Participant, 2-Cyl Ctr Gr Opn," 2000 Made, 5700PA, Exc-NIB $50-75**
☐ **ALSO SAME, Except "Canadian 2-Cylinder Club," NIB $65**
☐ **ALSO SAME, Except Gold Plated Presentation Model, NIB $250**

☐ **D, 1930, Vindex, CI, Nickeled Driver & Pulley, Excellent, $1800**
☐ **ALSO, REPRO, 1969, OTT, SCA, Excellent $35**
☐ **ALSO, REPRO, 1978, PTW, CA, WFE, NIB $35**
☐ **ALSO, REPRO, 1980, PC, CA, "Dalton MN," NIB $35**
☐ **ALSO, REPRO, 1988, ScaMo, CI, NIB $110**

☐ **D, 1970, Ertl, Die, WFE, Smooth Steel Rears Or On Rubber, Rivet Under Seat, Hole Or No Hole In Seat, Other Variations, Some Came In Closed Box, Stock No. 500, Custom, Excellent-NIB $20-25**
Notes:

☐ D, 1987, ScaMo, SCA, #15 In Collector Series, Limited To 5000, NIB $40
Notes:

☐ D, 1988, Dingman, Custom, Early Unstyled, With Spoke Flywheel, Excellent $300
Notes:

☐ D, 1989, Dingman, Custom, Styled, On Rubber Or Steel, With Hand Crank Or Electric Start, Excellent $270
☐ ALSO, Unstyled, On Rubber Or Steel, Excellent $285
Notes:

☐ D, 1989, Dingman, Custom, Gold 1937 Centennial Unstyled, 100 Made, Excellent $300
Notes:

☐ D, 1989, Keith, Custom, "Land Of Lincoln Show" Inscribed On Flywheel, NIB $80
Notes:

☐ D, 1990, Ertl, Die, Styled On Steel, Collector Edition, 5596DA, NIB $35
☐ ALSO SAME But On Rubber, Shelf, 5596DO, NIB $25
Notes:

☐ D, 1994, Ertl, Die, "Minnesota Division 1994," Green, 5718TA, NIB $50
☐ ALSO SAME, Except Gold, (See Color Plates), NIB $185
Notes:

☐ D, 1998, Ertl, Die, "Two-Cylinder Club Members," Spoke Flywheel, 5995TA, NIB $60
Notes:

☐ D, 1999, Ertl, Die, "75th Anniversary" Decal On Top Of Hood, 5178DA, NIB $40
Notes:

☐ D, 1999, Danbury Mint, Clock In Rear Wheel, NIB $65
Notes:

☐ D, 1999, Ertl, Die, 1925 Model D, 5179DO, NIB $20
Notes:

☐ G, 1983, Freiheit, CZ, Roll-O-Matic Front Axle, Excellent Detail, With Or Without Fenders, Excellent $300
Notes:

☐ G, 1983, ScaMo, NF, On Rubber, "Dyersville Show," Excellent-NIB $30-35
Notes:

☐ G, 1983, ScaMo, Die, NF, On Steel, No. 1 In JLE Collector Series II, 5000 Made, Excellent-NIB $30-40
☐ ALSO SAME, Except On Rubber, "1983 Dyersville Show," Excellent-NIB $30-40
Notes:

☐ G, 1987, Ertl, Die, Collector Insert, "50th Anniversary," On Steel, 548DA, Excellent-NIB $30-40
☐ ALSO, Shelf Model, 548DO, Excellent-NIB $15-20
Notes:

☐ G, 1991, C & M, Die, With Or Without Fenders, WFE Or N/F, Paul Stephan Pattern, Excellent $185
Notes:

☐ G, 1992, Riecke, Custom, N/F Or WFE, On Steel Or Rubber, With Or Without Fenders, Excellent $265
Notes:

☐ G, 1997, Ertl, Die, WFE, Collector Insert, Red Fuel Cap, 5103DA, NIB $50
☐ ALSO SAME, Except High Crop,"1997 2 Cylinder Club," 5000TA, NIB $70
Notes:

□ G, 1998, Ertl, Die, Styled, Steerable, 5104DO, NIB $28
Notes:

□ G, 2004, Ertl/RC, Die, Styled, Steerable, Rubber Tires, 15591, NIB $25
Notes:

□ GP, 1982, ScaMo, SCA, WF"3-10-84" Cast On Frame, Introduced At Lafayette Show, Excellent-NIB $35-40
□ ALSO SAME, Except "Rockford Illinois," "6-17-84" Cast In Frame, Excellent-NIB $35-40
□ ALSO SAME, But #9 JLE Coll. Series I, 3000 Made, Exc-NIB$35-40

□ GP, 1991, Dingman, Custom, Wide Tread, WFE, Side Steer Or Over-Hood Steer, Excellent $225
Notes:

□ GP, 1994, Ertl, Die, 1928-29 GP Standard, Collector Insert, 5767DA, Excellent-NIB $25-30
Notes:

□ GP, 1995, Ertl, Die, Standard, 1928-1935, Shelf Model, Modified Graphics And Air Cleaner, 5801DO, NIB $23
Notes:

□ GP, 1995, Ertl, Die, "Two Cylinder Club Potato Expo V," 5794TA, NIB $45
□ ALSO SAME, Except "Expo Participant," 5794, NIB $75
Notes:

□ GP, 1995, Ertl, Die, 1930 GP Wide Tread Tractor, 5787DO, NIB $22
Notes:

□ GP, 1996, Ertl, Die, 1931 Wide Tread, Insert, 5798DA, NIB $30
Notes:

□ H, 1988, NB & K, Custom, "Back East Show," 1800 Made, Serial Numbered, NIB $100
Notes:

□ H, 1989, Dingman, SCA, Options: Starter, Lights, Fenders, And W/F, NIB $165
Notes:

□ H, 1991, C & M, Die, WFE Or N/F, With or Without Fenders, Paul Stephan Pattern, NIB $130
Notes:

☐ **H, 2000, Ertl, Die, TBE15034, NIB $22**
Notes:

☐ **HN, 2000, Ertl, Die, Collector Edition, NIB $25**
Notes:

☐ **HWH, 1999, Ertl, Die, "Two Cylinder Club Exhibitor," NIB $100**
☐ **ALSO SAME, Except "Two Cylinder Club 1999," 16006A, NIB $70**
Notes:

☐ **L, 1990, SpecCast, Die, 5th *Toy Tractor Times* Tractor, 3450 Made, TTT010, NIB $45**
Notes:

☐ **L, 1994, 8th Anniversary of CTM (*Canadian Toy Menia* Magazine,) No Lights, NIB $45**
Notes:

☐ **L, 2001, SpecCast, Die, Unstyled, JDM 171, NIB $38**
Notes:

□ L, 2002, SpecCast, Die, Model "62," Round Fenders, 2nd In Series Of 6, JDM172, NIB $32
Notes:

□ L, 2002, SpecCast, Die, With John Deere Engine, Detailed With Levers And Pedals, 4th in "L" Series, JDM174, NIB $35
Notes:

□ LA, 1986, Riecke, Custom, Excellent $175
Notes:

□ LA, 1988, NB & K, Custom, Southern Indiana Show, 2300 Made, Serial Numbered, NIB $55
Notes:

□ LA, 1992, SpecCast, Die, "Great American Toy Show," CUST178, NIB $35
Notes:

□ LA, 1994, SpecCast, Die, JDM045, NIB $28
Notes:

☐ **LA, 2002, SpecCast, Die, Rubber Tires, Metal Rims, Levers, Pedals, 3rd In Series, NIB $30**
Notes:

☐ **M, 1986, Riecke, Custom, Rubber Tires, Excellent $160**
Notes:

☐ **M, 1989, Ertl, Die, "Series III Dubuque 1947-1952" Collector Insert, 540TA, Excellent-NIB $20-30**
☐ **ALSO SAME, Except Shelf Model, 540DO, $12-17**
Notes:

☐ **M, 1997, SpecCast, Die, Gold Edition, "50th Anniversary Dubuque Works," CUST433, NIB $65**
Notes:

☐ **MT, 1986, Riecke, Custom, Lever, Lights, Fan, Pedals, And Rubber Tires, Excellent $180**
Notes:

☐ **MT, 1995, SpecCast, Die, JDM056, NIB $32**
☐ **ALSO SAME, Except "5th Annual Crossroads Farm Toy Show," JDM056, NIB $40**
Notes:

☐ **MT, 1996, SpecCast, Die, WFE, JDM073, NIB $35**
Notes:

☐ **R, 1983, Trumm, SCA, Excellent-NIB $40-50**
Notes:

☐ **R, 1985, Ertl, Die, 2nd In Antique Series, Limited To 48 Per Dealer, 544DA, Excellent-NIB $30-40**
Notes:

☐ **R, 1985, Ertl, Die, WFE, Rubber Tires, With Or Without Green Stacks, 544TA, NIB $28**
Notes:

☐ **R, 1992, SC, Stephan, SC, Diesel, WFE, Highly Detailed, 750 Made, Custom, Excellent $265**
Notes:

☐ **WA-14, 1989, Trumm, SCA, 4WD, Without Cab, Excellent-NIB $400-450**
Notes:

☐ WA-14, 1989, Trumm, SCA, 4WD, With Cab, Excellent-NIB $500-600
Notes:

☐ WA-17, 1989, Trumm, SCA, 4WD, With Cab, NIB $650
Notes:

☐ WA-17, Krominga, Custom, $150
Notes:

☐ 40, 1990, Nolt, SC, Stephan Patterns, Custom, "8th Annual Back East Show," Limited To 1250, Serial Numbered, NIB $275.
Notes:

☐ 50, 1986, Standi, Plastic, Steerable, 250 WFE And 450 N/F Made, NIB $40
Notes:

☐ 50, 1997, Stephan, Custom, 500 Made, Limited Edition, Excellent $225
Notes:

☐ 55 Series, 1992, Ertl, Die, WFE, FWA, Cab, 5713, NIB $58
Notes:

☐ 60, 1955, Ertl, Die, NF, Taillight On Seat, Step-Down Rear Axle For Mounting Loader, Some With Paint Drain Hole Under Engine, Excellent-NIB $250-550
Notes:

☐ 60, 1993, Ertl, Die, LPG Orchard, Collector Insert, 5679DA, Excellent-NIB $25-32
☐ ALSO, SAME, Except "1993 Parts Expo," 5679DA, NIB $35
Notes:

☐ 60, 2001, Ertl/RC, Die, One Per Dealer, Black Seat, See-Through Engine Compartment, 15189, NIB $40
Notes:

☐ 60, 2001, Ertl/RC, Die, High Seat Model, "John Deere Expo XI Show Tractor," 16070A, NIB $75
☐ ALSO SAME, But "National Farm Toy Museum," NIB $75
☐ ALSO SAME, Except "National Farm Toy Museum Exhibitor," NIB $80

☐ 60, 2002, Ertl, Die, WFE, Or With Umbrella, "Iowa FFA 2002," Special Edition, 16096A, NIB $60
Notes:

☐ 70, 1991, Ertl, Die, Hi-Crop, WFE, 1991 Special Ed., 5611, NIB $35
Notes:

☐ 70, 1992, Ertl, Die, Row Crop, 5611, NIB $24
Notes:

☐ 70, 1995, Ertl, Die, Precision Classic #7, 5788CO, NIB $135
Notes:

☐ 70, 1996, Ertl, Die, "National Farm Toy Museum," Dyersville, IA, Or NF With Umbrella, 1219PA, NIB $50
Notes:

☐ 70, 1998, Ertl, Die, CE Iowa FFA, W/Umbrella, NIB $60
Notes:

☐ 70, 2000, Ertl, Die, Hi-Crop, National Farm Toy Museum, 16048A NIB $50
Notes:

☐ 70, 2003, Ertl/RC, Die, Precision Classic, No. 23, 1954-1956 Replica, Rubber Tires, Detailed Engine, Gold Collec. Medallion, Historical Booklet, TBE15366, NIB $120
Notes:

☐ 80, 1983, Trumm, SCA, Steerable, Rubber Tires, NIB $55
Notes:

☐ 80, 1992, Ertl, Die, "JD Columbus Commemorative," Green, 5704PA, Excellent-NIB $50-70
Notes:

☐ 80, 1992, Ertl, Die, "JD Columbus Commemorative," Gold Paint, 2275 Made, 5704YA, NIB $175
Notes:

☐ 80, 1993, Stephan, Custom, 500 Made, PSJ06, Excellent-NIB $275-300
Notes:

☐ 320, 1991, Stephan, Custom, "Back-East Show," 1250 Made (Nolt), Serial Nos., Excellent-NIB $200-250
Notes:

□ 320, 1991, Stephan, Custom, Geared Steering, 3 Pt. Hitch, Serial Numbered To 500, Excellent-NIB $200-265
Notes:

□ 330, 1989, NB & K, Custom, Decal, Ozarks Show, 658 Made, Rare, NIB $150
□ ALSO SAME, Except Unauthorized Spinoff, NIB $110
Notes:

□ 330, 1990, Trumm, Plastic, 10th Annual Plow City Show, NIB $45
Notes:

□ 330, 1993, Engle, SC, Custom, Lebanon Valley, NIB $165
Notes:

□ 430, 1958, Ertl, Die, 3-Pt., Stock #20, Excell-NIB $800-1900
□ ALSO SAME, But No 3 Pt., Excellent-NIB $850-2000
Notes:

□ 430, 1983, Nygren, SCA, 3 Point Hitch, Excellent Detail, NIB $165
Notes:

□ 435, 1988, NB & K, SC, Diesel, Custom, "Lebanon, PA, 1988" Show, 1500 Made, Serial Numbered, NIB $190
Notes:

□ 520, 1988, NB & K, Custom, Wheatland Style, Florida Show, NIB $100
Notes:

□ 520, 1986, Standi, Plastic, Steerable, 250 WFE And 450 N/F Made, NIB $45
Notes:

□ 520, 1997, Stephan, Custom, Serial Numbered, 350 Made, NF, NIB $260
Notes:

□ 520, 2002, Ertl/RC, Die, High Clearance Narrow Tractor, Single Front Wheel, "2002 2-Cylinder Club," 16089, NIB $70
Notes:

□ 520, 2002, Ertl/RC, WFE, Steerable, Rubber Tires, 15360, NIB $25
Notes

☐ **520, 2003, Ertl/RC, Die, Narrow Front, Rubber Tires, Steerable, 15599, NIB $27**
Notes:

☐ **530, 1986, Standi, Plastic, Steerable, 250 WFE And 450 N/F Made, NIB $48**
Notes:

☐ **530, 1991, Engle, Custom, "Lebanon Valley Show" Tractor, N/F, NIB $190**
Notes:

☐ **530, 2002, Nolt, WF, Limited to 250, Custom, NIB $200**
Notes:

☐ **620, 1955, Ertl, Die, NF, No 3 Point, Light On Rear Of Seat, On "60" Body, Excellent-NIB $350-900**
Notes:

☐ **620, 1956, Ertl, Die, 3 Pt Hitch, NF, No Lights Rear Of Seat, Excellent-NIB $400-1000**
☐ **ALSO SAME, Except Gold Plated, Scarce, Excellent $700**
Notes:

☐ 620, 1992, Ertl, Die, Orchard Tractor, "2-Cylinder Club Expo III," 5678, NIB $50
☐ ALSO SAME Except "Exhibitor Expo III 1992," Limited To 1000, 5678, NIB $100
Notes:

☐ 620, 2001, Ertl/RC, High-Crop, Collector Edition, 15188A, NIB $65
Notes:

☐ 620, 2002, Ertl/RC, Die, Limited Edition, 2002 "Summer Farm Toy Show," 16091A, NIB $65
☐ ALSO, SAME Except "Exhibitor," 16091A, NIB $90
Notes:

☐ 620, 2002, Ertl/RC, Die, WF, TBE-15428, NIB $40
Notes:

☐ 630, 1958, Ertl, Die, NF, 3 point, Some Have "430" Decals On Hood, Stock No 10, Excellent-NIB $400-750
☐ ALSO SAME, Except "630" Decals On Hood, Excellent-NIB $350-700
Notes:

☐ 630, 1959, Ertl, Die, No 3 Point, Smooth Or Ribbed Front Tires, NF, Stock No. 10, Excellent-NIB $350-900
☐ ALSO SAME, Except No Muffler Hole, Excellent-NIB $800-1800
Notes:

☐ 630, 2002, Ertl/RC, Die, High Crop, 2,500 Made, "John Deere Collectors' Center," Precision Series, 15427A, NIB $500
Notes:

☐ 630, 2002, Ertl/RC, Die, RC Precision Classic #21, TBE15364, NIB $110
Notes:

☐ 630 LP, 1988, Ertl , Die, "11th National Farm Toy Show Tractor," 5590PA, NIB $50
Notes:

☐ 630 LP, 1989, Ertl, Die, "1989 Special Edition JD 630 LP," 5590DA, NIB $30
☐ ALSO SAME, Except Shelf Model, 5590DO, NIB $30
Notes:

☐ 720, 1990, Ertl, Die, Hi-Crop, "2 Cylinder Club Expo II 1990," 10,000 Made, 5610TA, NIB $75
☐ ALSO SAME, Except "Special Edition, Open Box, 5610DA, NIB $38
Notes:

☐ 720, 1991, Yoder, Plastic, Diesel, NF, Pony Motor Starter, 1260 Made, Excellent-NIB $50-65
☐ ALSO SAME Except WFE, 1195 Made, Excellent-NIB $50-65
☐ ALSO SAME, Except 1990, Electric Starter, 3236 Made, Excellent NIB $50-65
☐ ALSO SAME Except WFE Electric Starter, 3488 Made, Excellent-NIB $50-65

□ 720, 1993, Yoder, Plastic, Standard, With Adjustable Front Axle & 3pt, Excellent-NIB $50-65
□ ALSO SAME, Except Pony Starter, Excell-NIB $50-75
□ ALSO SAME, Except Electric Start, Excel-NIB $50-75
Notes:

□ 720, 1994, Ertl, Die, Row Crop, "*Toy Tractor Times* Anniversary 1994," 5844TA, NIB $55
Notes:

□ 720, 1996, Ertl, Die, Precision Classic #10, 5832CO, NIB $125
Notes:

□ 720, 1997, Ertl, Die, Detailed, With Authentic Graphics, 5007DO, NIB $32
Notes:

□ 720, 2001, Ertl/RC, Die, Gas, With Loader, Blade, Chains, Weather Brake, Canvas Enclosure, Precision Classic No 18, 15165, NF, Stock No 10, NIB $115
Notes:

□ 730, 1958, Sigomec, Die, Argentina, With Or W/O Air Breather & 3pt, Very Rarely Seen, NIB $1200
□ ALSO SAME, 1992 Recast, NA
Notes:

□ 730, 1987, Yoder, Plastic, 1987 Lafayette Show, N/F, 4100 Made, NIB $85
Notes:

□ 730, 1988, Yoder, Plastic, 1988 Lafayette Show, WFE, 4400 Made, Excellent-NIB $70-90
Notes:

□ 730, 1990, Yoder, Plastic, 1993 Plow City Show Tractor, NIB $70
Notes:

□ 730, 1992, Engle, Custom, 730 Standard, Lebanon Valley Toy Show, NIB $250
□ ALSO SAME, Except LP, NIB $250
Notes:

□ 730, Danbury Mint, Clock In Rear Wheel, NIB $55
Notes:

□ 730, 1995, Yoder, Plastic, 1995 Goshen Show, Diesel, With Adjustable Front Axle, NIB $75
Notes:

☐ 730, 1998, Ertl, Die, Precision Classic #13 NF, 5766CO, NIB $135
Notes:

☐ 820, 1983, Trumm, SCA, Same As 80, But With Decal, Excellent-NIB $55-60
Notes:

☐ 820, 1991, Stephan, Custom, 500 Made, PSJD01, Excellent-NIB $350-465
Notes:

☐ 820, 1993, Ertl, Die, Diesel, W/F, Stock #, 5705DO, Excellent-NIB $20-30
☐ ALSO SAME, Except, 1994, "Western Minnesota Steam Thresher Reunion," 100 Made, NIB $100

☐ 830, 1983, Trumm, SCA, Similar To 820 Trumm, Fat Muffler, NIB $85
Notes:

☐ 830, 1990, Stephan, Custom, 500 Made, Excellent-NIB $400-550
Notes:

□ 830, Trumm, SCA, Canadian Show Tractor, "Watsons-Weyburn" Embossed On Flywheel, NIB $100
Notes:

□ 950, 1985, Ertl, Die, Utility With ROPS, FWA, Muffler Stop Supports Muffler, 581, Excellent-NIB $10-17
□ ALSO SAME Except No Muffler Stop, NIB $35
Notes:

□ 950, 2000, Ertl, Die, TBE15163, NIB $17
Notes:

□ 1010, 1999, Stephan, Custom, "*Toy Tractor Times*," NIB $275
Notes:

□ 2010, 1973, Ertl, Die, Utility, Old Nose, Excell-NIB $42-55
□ ALSO SAME Except W/Loader, Excell-NIB $80-125
Notes:

□ 2010, 1989, NB & K, Custom, "3rd Annual Florida Show," 1400 Made, NIB $165
Notes:

☐ 2030, '76, Ertl, Die, Utility, Solid Yellow Decal, Old Nose, 516, NIB $50
☐ ALSO SAME, Except With Loader, Variations In Loader Levers And Rivets, 592, NIB $90
☐ ALSO SAME, Except New Generation Hood, Split Or Solid Frame, Other Variations, 584, NA

☐ 2040, 1980, Ertl, Die, Utility, Strobe Decal, 516, Excellent-NIB $12-17
☐ ALSO SAME Except With Loader, W/Loader, 517, NIB $30
Notes:

☐ 2440, 1980, Ertl, Die, Seat And Loader Hole Variations, 516, NIB $20
Notes:

☐ 2440, 1980, Ertl, Die, WFE, Utility, With Loader, Generation II Hood, Riveted Or Spun-On Front Wheels, 517, NIB $27
Notes:

☐ 2440, 2000, Ertl, Die, TBE15161, NIB $18
Notes:

☐ 2440, 2000, Ertl, Die, With Loader, TBE15162, NIB $22
Notes:

☐ 2520, 1994, ScaMo, Die, Farm Progress Days, FB-2154, NIB $70
Notes:

☐ 2550, 1983, Ertl, Die, Collector Series, Decal Has 2550, 24 Allowed Per Dealer, 501DA, NIB $40
Notes:

☐ 2550, 1985, Ertl, Die, Utility, FWA, Cab, Loader, 503, Excellent-NIB $25-35
☐ ALSO SAME But No Loader, 501, Excell-NIB $17-25
Notes:

☐ 2640, 1990, Ertl, Die, Collector Insert, "Field Of Dreams," 516DA, NIB $28
Notes:

☐ 2755, 1989, Ertl, Die, Cab, FWA, With Loader, With Or Without Pin In Loader Shaft, Large Or Small Front Wheel Drive Shaft, 5578DO, Excellent-NIB $25-35
☐ ALSO SAME But No Loader, 5579DO, Excell-NIB $20-30
Notes:

☐ 3010, 1961, Ertl, Die, NF, Die Cast Rims, Without 3pt, No Fuel Filters, Stock No 30, Excellent-NIB $225-475
☐ ALSO SAME, Except With 3-Point, Exc-NIB $175-450
☐ SAME, Except Gold-Plated Dealer Award, Excellent $600
Notes:

□ 3010, 1992, Ertl, Die, Shelf Model, Black Seat, 5635DO, NIB $22
Notes:

□ 3010, 1992, Ertl, Die, Collector Edition, WFE, Yellow Seat, Error On Engine (Gasoline One Side, Diesel Other), 5635DA, NIB $35
Notes:

□ 3010, Ertl/RC, Die, Precision Classic, No 20, 15210, NIB $105
Notes:

□ 3010, 2000, ScaMo, Die, Beckman High School, NIB $50
Notes:

□ 3020, '64, ED, Short Filters, Die Rims, N/F, No 3 Pt, Excellent-NIB $125-300
□ ALSO SAME But Plastic Rims, 4 Lvers, Exc-NIB $100-250
□ ALSO SAME But W/3 Point, Boy Box, Exc-NIB $160-370
□ SAME, Wide Rear Rims, WFE, ROPS, Bble Bx, Exc-NIB $255-400

□ 3020, 1965, Ertl, Die, Plastic Rims, Short Filters, Wide Front End, ROPS, Excellent-NIB $225-400
□ ALSO SAME But No ROPS, Excellent-NIB $140-250
Notes:

□ **3020, 1969, Ertl, Die, Plastic Rims, Long Filters, 530, Excellent-NIB $70-160**
Notes

□ **3020, 1969, Ertl, Die, Plastic Rims, Long Filters, WFE With ROPS, Excellent-NIB $200-400**
□ **ALSO SAME But No ROPS, Excellent-NIB $130-240.**
Notes:

□ **3020, 1987, ScaMo, Die, NF, "10th Nat'l Farm Toy Show," NIB $25**
□ **ALSO SAME, Except 1988, "11th National Farm Toy Show," Metallic Green, NIB $30**
□ **ALSO SAME, Except 1989, "12th Annual Fall Toy Show," NIB $30**

□ **ALSO SAME, Except 1990, "13th National Farm Toy Show," Excellent $200**

□ **3020, 1993, Custom, RC, "Benninger 6th Formosa, Canada, Toy Show," NIB $110**
Notes:

□ **3020, 1994, Ertl, Die, Wide Front, "1994 Summer Toy Show," 5059TA, NIB $50**
Notes:

□ **3020, 1995, Ertl, Die, "Summer Farm Toy Show Exhibitor," 5059, NIB $80**
Notes:

□ **3020, 2003, Ertl/RC, Die, TBE15483, NIB $30**
Notes:

□ **3030, Ertl, Die, ROPS, Bubble Box, 533, NIB $425**
Notes:

□ **4000, 1994, Ertl, Die, ROPS, Precision Classic, 5684CO, NIB $165**
Notes:

□ **4010, 1993, Ertl, Die, ROPS, "National Farm Toy Show," 5716PA, NIB $55**
Notes:

□ **4010, 1994, Ertl, Die, Row Crop, Gas, Collector Edition, 5716DA, Excellent-NIB $30-36**
□ **ALSO SAME, Except Diesel, WFE, 5716DO, NIB $30**
Notes:

□ **4010, 2000, Danbury Mint, Porcelain, Clock In Rear Wheel, NIB $50**
Notes:

□ 4010, 1997, Ertl, Die, "Wisconsin Farm Progress Days," NIB $85
Notes:

□ 4010, 1997, Ertl, Die, 5716DP, Excellent-NIB $20-25
□ ALSO SAME, Except "Fort Plain FFA 1998 Show Tractor," 150 Made NIB $75
Notes:

□ 4010, 1999, Ertl, Die, "Iowa State Fair '99," With Umbrella, 3500 Made, 16028A, NIB $100
Notes:

□ 4010, 2000, Ertl, Die, With Hiniker Cab, "40th Anniversary Collector Edition," 15111A, NIB $50
Notes:

□4020, Parker, 6-Cylinder Tractor, ROPS, NIB $150
Notes:

□ 4020, 1990, C & M, Custom, Several Options, W/Cab, ROPS, Or No Cab, N/F, Excellent-NIB $190-225
□ SAME, Except 1991, 25th Annual National Pulling Championship, 500 Made, Excellent-NIB $170-200
Notes:

☐ 4020, 1992, Ertl, Die, Precision Classic, 3rd In Series, 5638CO, NIB $160
☐ 4020, 1992, Ertl, Die, Diesel, FFA Limited Edition, Precision Classic, 4992RO, NIB $400
Notes:

☐ 4020, 1999, Ertl, Die, Precision Model With 237 Corn Picker, 5083KO, NIB $165
Notes:

☐ 4020, 1993, Ertl, Die, Precision Classic, WFE, 5549CO, Excellent-NIB $300-475
Notes:

☐ 4020, Ertl, Die, WFE, Wide Rear Tires, ROPS, All Have 4020 Decals On 30 Series Bodies, NIB $375
Notes:

☐ 4020, Ertl, Die, Narrow Front, Wide Rear Tires, (Repainted Model Shown), NIB $240
Notes:

☐ 4040, 1999, Ertl, Die, 5133, NIB $30
Notes:

□ 4040, 2003, Ertl/RC, Die, Duals, No Cab, Steerable, TBE15478, NIB $40
Notes:

□ 4230, 1978, Sigomec, Die, WFE, No Cab, 3 Pt, Argentina, 2512, Duals, Stock 2515, (Ertl Model Shown) NIB $100
Notes:

□ 4230, 1998, Ertl, Die, "21st National Farm Toy Show" Tractor, 5507AA, NIB $60
□ ALSO SAME, Except Gold (SEE COLOR PLATES)
Notes:

□ 4230, 1999, Ertl, Die, Collector Version, 5132DA, NIB $48
Notes:

□ 4230, 2002, Ertl, Die, FWA, Steerable, Two Steps To Platform, 15202, NIB $33
Notes: :

□ 4250, 1982, Ertl, Die, "5th National Show" Tractor, 1550 Made, 5507AA, NIB $500
Notes:

☐ **4255, 1989, Ertl, Die, Cab, Balloon Front Tires, 5583DO, NIB $50**
Notes:

☐ **4430, 1972, Ertl, Die, Cab, Filler Caps, Plain Box, 512, NIB $110**
☐ **Also SAME, Except In Slick Box, NIB $125**
Notes:

☐ **4430, 1973, Sigomec, Die, Fenders, 3pt, No Cab, With Or Without Duals, NIB $100**
Notes:

☐ **4440, 1979, Ertl, Die, Strobe Decal, Cab, Duals, 542, Excellent-NIB $55-70**
Notes:

☐ **4440, 1979, Ertl, Die, Strobe Decal, Cab, Single Rears, Brown Seat, 512, Excellent-NIB $50-65**
Notes:

☐ **4440, 1980, Or 1987, Ertl, Plastic, Cab, Radio Controlled, With Or Without Front Weights, 31 Or 31CO, Excellent-NIB $50-65**
Notes:

☐ 4440, 1995, Ertl, Die, "Iowa State Fair Blue Ribbon Foundation," Limited Edition, Laser Etching And Serialization, 3,500 Made, 5820TA, NIB $125
Notes:

☐ 4440 2000, Ertl, Die, Precision Classic, TBE15077, NIB $110
☐ ALSO SAME, Except Sold Under "Hamilton Authenticated" Name, 98406, NIB $110
Notes:

☐ 4440, Ertl, Die, No Filler Caps, Solid Yellow Decal, NF, 512, NIB $70
Notes:

☐ 4450, 1982, Ertl, Die, Green Cab, Plastic Exhaust & A/C, 5506, Excellent-NIB $40-50
Notes:

☐ 4450, 1982, Ertl, Die, Green Cab, Plastic Exhaust & A/C, Balloon Front Tires, Duals, 5507, Excellent-NIB $45-60
Notes:

☐ 4450, 1989, Ertl, Die, WFE, Cab, Push-On Fronts, 541, NIB $30
☐ ALSO SAME, Black Cab, Duals, 541, Exc-NIB $22-30
Notes:

☐ **4450, 1987, Ertl, Die, Limited Edition, Insert, Commemorative For JD Syracuse Branch, 541TA, NIB $75**
Notes:

☐ **4450, 1996, Ertl, Die, Replica 15th Anniversary, Laser-Etched, 2544PA, NIB $75**
Notes:

☐ **4450, 2000, Ertl, Die, TBE15160, NIB $25**
Notes:

☐ **4455, 1989, Ertl, Die, FWA, Cab, 5584, NIB $45**
Notes:

☐ **4520, 2001, Ertl/RC, Die, "2001 National Farm Toy Show," Hiniker Cab, NIB $80**
☐ **ALSO SAME, Except Gold-Plated (See Color Section)**
☐ **ALSO SAME, Except Collector Edition, 15646, NIB $55**
Notes:

☐ **4620, 2002, Ertl/RC, Die, ROPS, TBE15283, NIB $45**
☐ **ALSO SAME, Except Collector Edition, 15282A, NIB $45**
Notes:

☐ **4620, 2004, Ertl/RC, 200th Birthday, Hiniker Cab, TBE15646A, NA**
Notes:

☐ **4760, 2002, Ertl/RC, Die, With MFWD, TBE15349, NIB $35**
Notes:

☐ **4850, 1982, Ertl, Die, "New Orleans 7-82 Collectors Series," FWA, Has "4850" On Decal, 584-DA, NIB $100**
Notes:

☐ **4850, 1985, Ertl, Die, FWA, Cab, Duals, Front Weights, Variations, No "4850" On Decal, 584, NIB $48**
☐ **ALSO SAME, Except With "4850" On Side Decal, NIB $48**
Notes:

☐ **4955, 1989, Ertl, Die, FWA, Cab, Duals, 5587, NIB $58**
Notes:

☐ **4960, 1992, Ertl, Die, FWA, Cab, 5709CO, NIB $50**
Notes:

□ 5010, 2004, Ertl/RC, Die, Precision Classics, 1/16, TBE15608, NA

□ 5020, 1969, Ertl, Die, No Front Axle Brace, One Piece Aircleaner, Closed Box, 555, Excellent-NIB $90-185
Notes:

□ 5020, 1970, Ertl, Die, Open Front Axle Braces, And 2 Piece Air Cleaner, (Non-Tapered Pole), 555, Excellent-NIB $70-125
Notes:

□ 5020, Krominga, Custom, Excellent-NIB $225-275
Notes:

□ 5020, 1971, Ertl, Die, Solid Or Open Front Axle Braces, No Air-Cleaner, Green Box, 555, Excellent-NIB $45-65
Notes:

□ 5020, 1972, Ertl, Die, No Air Cleaner And Long Side Decals, 555, Excellent-NIB $60-75
Notes:

☐ **5020, 1986, Ertl, Die, Same, But Push Nut Front Wheels, 555DO, Excellent-NIB $40-60**
Notes:

☐ **5020, 1987, Ertl, Die, "First Canadian International Farm Equipment Show," "1837-1987 John Deere 150" On Medallion On Side Of Hood, Excell-NIB $170-235**
Notes:

☐ **5020, 1991, Ertl, Die, "1991 National Farm Toy Museum," Duals, 555PA, NIB $135**
Notes:

☐ **5020, Reschke, Custom, ROPS, NIB $85**
Notes:

☐ **5200, 1995, Ertl, Die, ROPS, Collector Insert, 5845DA, NIB $27**
Notes:

☐ **5400, 1995, Ertl, Die, ROPS, WFE, 5846DO, NIB $24**
☐ **ALSO SAME, Except 1997, Revised, 5846DP, NIB $24**
Notes:

☐ 5420, 2002, Ertl/RC, Die, With Model 541 Loader, Raises, Lowers, Dumps, Steerable, TBE 15357, NIB $35
Notes:

☐ 6030, Reschke, No Cab, Custom, NIB $155
Notes:

☐ 6030, Reschke, Cab, Custom, NIB $265
Notes:

☐ 6030, Reschke, Cab, Rice Tires, Custom, NIB $265
Notes:

☐ 6200, 1994, Ertl, Die, FWA, WFE, ROPS, Shelf Model, 5667DO, Excellent-NIB $15-22
☐ ALSO SAME, But 2WD, 5666DO, Excell-NIB $15-22
Notes:

☐ 6230, Krominga, Custom, Excellent-NIB $225-275
Notes:

☐ 6400, 1993, Ertl, Die, Special Edition, MFWD And ROPS, 5667DA, Excellent-NIB $22-30
☐ ALSO SAME, No MFWD, 5666DA, Exc-NIB $22-30
Notes:

☐ 6400, Bruder-Firth, Plastic, Germany, NIB $8
Notes:

☐ 6400, 1996, Ertl, Die, With Loader, 5916CO, NIB $35
Notes:

☐ 6410, 1999, Ertl, Die, With Loader, 5069, NIB $32
Notes:

☐ 6420, Ertl/RC, Die, TBE15208, With Or Without Loader, Brown Interior, NIB $35
Notes:

☐ 7020, 1990, Precision Engineering, Plastic, 4WD, Articulated, Cab, 100 Made, Various Colors, Custom, NIB $400
Notes:

□ 7520, 1972, Ertl, Die, Cab, 4WD, One-Piece Straight Or Tapered Air Cleaner, Cab Rivet Or No Cab Rivet, 510, Excellent-NIB $300-500
Notes:

□ 7520, 1975, Ertl, Die, No Air Cleaner, 510, Excellent-NIB $600-1000
Notes:

□ 7520, 1990, Precision Engineering, Custom, NIB $400
□ ALSO SAME, Except "Central Ohio Farm Show Tractor, NIB $400
Notes:

□ 7600, 1994, Ertl, Die, WFE, Shelf Model, NIB $30
Notes:

□ 7610, 2000, Ertl, Die, With MFWD, TBE15128, NIB $32
Notes:

□ 7800, 1992, Ertl, Die, FWA, Kit, "Waterloo Introduction," 1 Per Dealer, 2900 Made, 5681QA, NIB $110
□ ALSO SAME, Except "Mannheim (Germany) Introduction" One Per Dealer In Europe, 3500 Made, 5717QA, NIB $100

□ 7800, 1992, Ertl, Die, FWA, Kit, "Demonstrator," 5719BO, $35-45
□ ALSO SAME, Except "Employee," 5718QA, NIB $70
□ ALSO SAME, Except "Dealership Tractor," 5739BO, NIB $45
Notes:

□ 7800, 1992, Ertl, Die, FWA And Duals, Collector Edition, 5619CA, NIB $40
□ ALSO SAME, Except Premier Edition, Different Castings Than Other No. 5619s, 5619CA, NIB $40
Notes:

□ 7800, 1992, Ertl, Die, Duals, Collector Edition, 5627CA, NIB $40
Notes:

□ 7800, 1993, Ertl, Die, WFE, MFWD, Cab, Premier Edition, Detailed Interior, Front Weights, 5627DO, Excellent-NIB $25-40
Notes:

□ 7810, 1997, Ertl, Die, "Ohio Young Farmers 50th Anniversary," "OYF" Logo On Side Of Hood, No Ertl Stock Number, NIB $75
□ ALSO SAME, But No Logo, MFWD, PM5200, NIB $75
Notes:

□ 8010, 1989, Trumm, SCA, 4WD, No Cab, Excellent-NIB $400-500
Notes:

□ 8020, 1989, Trumm, SCA, 4WD, No Cab, (Normally Has A Muffler), Excellent-NIB $400-500
Notes:

□ 8020, 2002, Ertl/RC, Die, "Precision Classic No. 22," 1960-64 Replica, Detailed Engine And Control Console, Grille And Battery Compartments Open, Working 3-Point, Swinging Drawbar, Medallion, Booklet, TBE15365, NIB $145

□ 8200, 1995, Ertl, Die, 5840CP, Excellent-NIB $25-34
□ ALSO SAME, Except 1997, Updated Graphics, Excellent-NIB $25-35
Notes:

□ 8200, 1997, Ertl, PL, Remote Control, 5196, NIB $60
□ ALSO SAME, Except TBE5052, NIB $55
Notes:

□ 8210, 2000, Ertl, Plastic, Radio Control, TBE36135, NIB $65
Notes:

□ 8210, 2003, Ertl/RC, Die, Large Tires, Steerable, TBE15476, NIB $50
Notes:

☐ 8300, 1995, Ertl, Die, Shelf Model, Single Rear Wheels, 5786CO, Excellent-NIB $25-35
Notes:

☐ 8300, 1996, Ertl, Die, FWA, Shelf, Updated Hood, Wrap Decals, Hi-Horsepower, 5786CP, Excellent-NIB $25-35
Notes:

☐ 8300, 1997, Ertl, Plastic, Remote Control, 5197, NIB $60
Notes:

☐ 8300T, 1999, Ertl, Die, 5182, Excellent-NIB $30-40
Notes:

☐ 8310, 2000, Ertl, Die, MFD, "1999 Farm Progress Show," 15117A, NIB $150
Notes:

☐ 8310, 2000, Ertl, Plastic, Radio Control, TBE36135, NIB $65
Notes:

□ 8310T, 2000, Ertl, Die, TBE15072, NIB $42
Notes:

□ 8400, 1994, Ertl, Die, Collector Edition, Duals, Plastic Front Fenders, 5786CA, NIB $65
Notes:

□ 8400T, 1998, Ertl, Die, No Waterloo Decals, "JD 8400T/Collector Edition 1999," 5181CA, NIB $68
□ ALSO SAME, Except "Waterloo Works 80th Anniversary," 5176CA, NIB $250
Notes:

□ 8410, Ertl, Die, 15061, NIB $35
Notes

□ 8420, Ertl/RC, Die, Row Crop, Duals, MFWD, TBE15200, NIB $45
Notes:

□ 8420T, Ertl/RC, Die, Tracked Tractor, MFWD, TBE15207, NIB $45
Notes:

☐ 8430, 1991, Ertl, Die, Ertl Customized, "Elmira Toy Celebration, Canada," NIB $175
Notes:

☐ 8520, 2002, Ertl/RC, Die, Triples On Rear, Collector Series, NIB $70
Notes:

☐ 8520, 2002, Ertl/RC, Die, European Tractor, TBE15406, NIB $45
Notes:

☐ Logos and information can be found almost anywhere on farm toys. Ertl placed identifying information about their John Deere R, made in 1985, around the flywheel. The leaping deer, difficult to see, is in the white center of the toy.

☐ 8560, 1988, Ertl, Die, 4WD, Cab, Duals, 5595, Excellent-NIB $65-90
Notes:

☐ 8630, 1975, Ertl, Die, 4WD, Cab, Duals, 597, Excellent-NIB $110-165
Notes:

☐ 8640, 1980, Ertl, Die, 4WD, Cab, Duals, Strobe Decal, 597, Excellent-NIB $100-150
Notes:

☐ 8640, 1981, Ertl, Die, 50 Series Cab With Small Windows (Just Above Front Wheels), 1323 Stamped On Box, 597, NIB $200
Notes: :

☐ 8520, Ertl/RC, Die, European Tr., TBE15406, NIB $45
Notes:

☐ 8650, 1982, Ertl, Die, 4 WD, Duals, "Collector Series July 1982," With Model Number Decal, 5508CA, Excellent-NIB $125-185
Notes:

☐ 8650, 1983, Ertl, Die, WFE, 4WD, Cab, Articulated, Duals, 5508CO, Excellent-NIB $70-85
Notes:

☐ 8650, 1991, Gottman, Die, Kinze Power Conversion, 4WD, NIB $800
Notes:

☐ 8760, 1988, Ertl, Die, Insert, 4WD, Spec Ed, 5595BA, NIB $65
Notes:

☐ 8760, 1992, Ertl, Die, 4WD, Articulated, 5715BO, NIB $70
Notes:

☐ 8870, 1994, Ertl, Die, 5762BO, NIB $75
Notes:

☐ 8960, 1988, Ertl, Die, Denver Limited Edition, September 1988, 2000 Made, 5595NA, Excellent-NIB $400-600
Notes:

☐ 9200, 1998, Ertl, Die, Triples, 15009, NIB $80
Notes:

☐ 9200, Precision Engineering, Custom, NIB $175
Notes:

9300, 1997, Die, Ertl, 4WD, PM5915, NIB $75
Notes:

□ 9300T, 2000, Ertl, Die, TBE-15007, NIB $60
Notes:

□ 9400T, 2000, Ertl, Die, Collector Edition, 15005A, NIB $70
□ ALSO SAME Except Employee Edition, NIB $150
Notes:

□ 9420, 2002, Ertl, Die, 4X4, Duals, 15205, NIB $70
Notes:

□ 9420T, 2002, Ertl, Die, 15206, NIB $65
Notes:

□ 9520, 2003, Ertl/RC, Die, Row Crop, Triples, 1/16, TBE15479, NA
Notes:

☐ **A, 2000, ScaMo, SC, Styled, JLE1016, 5917, NIB $150**
Notes:

Begin 1/8 Scale

☐ **B, 1996, ScaMo, SCA, NF, On Rubber, Steerable, FY-1000, NIB $150**
☐ **ALSO SAME, Except WFE, 1010, NIB $150**
☐ **ALSO SAME, Except "1998 Farm Progress Show," FB-2504, NIB $150**
Notes:

☐ **BW, 2000, ScaMo, WF, JLE-1010A, NIB $150**
Notes:

☐ **D, 1998, ScaMo, SCA, On Rubber, Spoke Wheels, FY-1008, NIB $140**
Notes:

☐ **70, 1997, ScaMo, Die, FY-1005, NIB $140**
Notes:

☐ **4010, 2000, ScaMo, SC, NF, Diesel, 1011, NIB $145**
☐ **ALSO SAME, Except NF, JLE1011A, NIB $145**
☐ **ALSO SAME, Except "Summer Toy Festival," NIB $145**
Notes:

☐ **4020, 2001, ScaMo, SC, WF, NIB $165**
Notes:

☐ **A, 1978, Kruse, Wood, NF, Styled Version On Rubber, Or Unstyled On Steel, Custom, Rarely Seen & Impossible To Price Accurately**
Notes:

Begin 1/10 Scale

☐ **B, 1980, Kruse, Wood, NF, Steel Wheels, Also Styled Version On Rubber, Custom, Rarely Seen & Impossible To Price Accurately**
Notes:

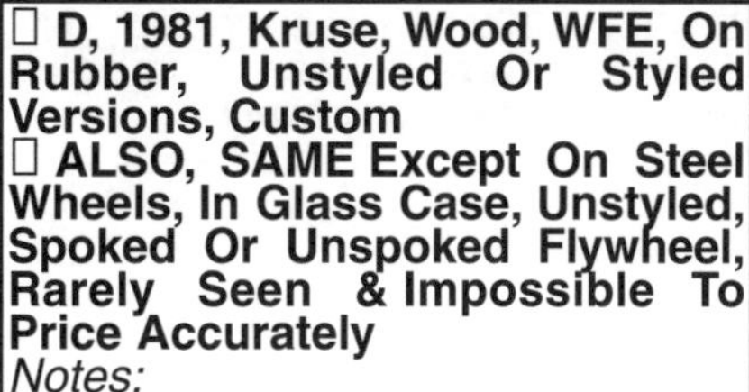

☐ D, 1981, Kruse, Wood, WFE, On Rubber, Unstyled Or Styled Versions, Custom
☐ ALSO, SAME Except On Steel Wheels, In Glass Case, Unstyled, Spoked Or Unspoked Flywheel, Rarely Seen & Impossible To Price Accurately
Notes:

☐ G, 1981, Kruse, Wood, NF, Various Wheel Styles, Also Unstyled Version, Custom, Rarely Seen & Impossible To Price Accurately *Notes:*

☐ GP, 1978, Kruse, Wood, NF or WFE, Steel Wheels, Custom, Rarely Seen & Impossible To Price Accurately
Notes:

☐ L, 1982, Kruse, Wood, NF, On Rubber, Styled Or Unstyled, Custom, Rarely Seen & Impossible To Price Accurately
Notes:

☐ R, 1982, Kruse, Wood, NF, Custom, Rarely Seen & Impossible To Price Accurately
Notes:

☐ 50, 1983, Kruse, Wood, NF, Custom, Rarely Seen & Impossible To Price Accurately
Notes:

☐ 60, 1984, Kruse, Wood, NF, Custom, Rarely Seen & Impossible To Price Accurately
Notes:

☐ 70, Kruse, Wood, NF, Custom, Rarely Seen & Impossible To Price Accurately
Notes:

☐ 80, 1982, Kruse, Wood, NF, Custom, Rarely Seen & Impossible To Price Accurately
Notes:

□ 430, 1984, Kruse, Wood, WFE, Custom, Rarely Seen & Impossible To Price Accurately
Notes:

□ 520, 1983, Kruse, Wood, NF, Custom, Rarely Seen & Impossible To Price Accurately
Notes:

□ 530, 1983, Kruse, Wood, NF, Custom, Rarely Seen & Impossible To Price Accurately
Notes:

□ 620, 1984, Kruse, Wood, NF, Custom, Rarely Seen & Impossible To Price Accurately
Notes:

□ 630, 1984, Kruse, Wood, WF, Custom, Rarely Seen & Impossible To Price Accurately
Notes:

□ 720, 1982, Kruse, Wood, Gas, NF, Custom, Rarely Seen & Impossible To Price Accurately
Notes:

□ 730, 1983, Kruse, Wood, NF Or WFE, With Or Without Fenders, Custom
□ ALSO SAME, Except WFE, Wheatland, Rarely Seen & Impossible To Price Accurately
Notes:

□ 820, 1984, Kruse, Wood, WFE, Custom, Rarely Seen & Impossible To Price Accurately
Notes:

□ 830, 1979, Kruse, Wood, WFE, Custom, Rarely Seen & Impossible To Price Accurately
Notes:

☐ A, 1975, Gray, CA/Korloy, NF, Custom, Steel Wheels, Crude, Excellent $35
☐ ALSO SAME, Except 1978, PTW, On Rubber, Robert Gray Molds, $40
☐ ALSO SAME, Except A, 1980, OTC, CA, NF, On Steel Or Rubber, Or "Mankato Show" (100 Made), Excellent $40

Begin 1/12 Scale

☐ GP, 1985, Price, Cast Iron, NF, Steel Wheels, Crude, Some Red, Some With "Deere" Misspelled, Robert Gray Copy, Taiwan, Larger Than Gray Original, 5152, $10
Notes:

☐ 8570, 1998, Valley Sand Cast Models, SCA, NIB $400
☐ ALSO, SAME Body Except 8570 Decal, NIB $400
☐ ALSO, SAME Except 8870 Decal, NIB $400
☐ ALSO, SAME Except 8970 Decal, NIB $400
Notes:

☐ A, 1950, Arcor, Rubber or Vinyl, Various Greens, Never Found NIB, Excellent $20
Notes:

Begin 1/20 Scale

☐ M Or MT, 1950, Arcor, Rubber or Vinyl, Green, Wheel Variations, Color Variations, NIB $20
Notes:

☐ 4430, 1973, Ertl, Plastic, Kit, Cab, Duals, 3 Pt, NIB $50
☐ ALSO SAME, EXCEPT 1999, Reissue In New Box, $15
Notes:

Begin 1/25 Scale

☐ A, 1950s, Auburn, Rubber, Various Colors, Including Green, Excellent $12
Notes:

Begin 1/32 Scale

☐ B, 1981, Brown, Lead, Unstyled, WFE, NF, or Single Front Wheel, Represents 1935-1938 Model, Kit, NIB $35
Notes:

☐ B, 1981, Brown, Lead, Styled, WFE, NF, or Single Front Wheel, Represents 1935-1938 Model, NIB $35
Notes:

□ Telehandler, 2002, Ertl/RC, Die, TBE40062, NIB $35
Notes:

□ 3020, Lee Toys, Die, NF, Red And Silver Or Green, Custom, NIB $10
□ ALSO SAME, Except Red And Silver With Brown Cab or Red With Red Cab, Custom, NIB $12
Notes:

□ 3140, Ertl, Die, Removable Metal Cab, MFWD, 5696, NIB $12
Notes:

□ 3140, 1980, Ertl, Die, FWA, Wheel Variations, European Square Cab, H1635 Or 1635, Excellent-NIB $15-20
Notes:

□ 3140, 1981, WFE, FWA, Utility, Rear Wheels Spun On, 5512, Excellent-NIB $6-12
□ ALSO SAME, Except Sound Guard Cab, Muffler Or No Muffer, Black Plastic Snap On Hitch Or Not, 5512, Excellent-NIB $8-12
Notes:

□ 3140, 1989, Ertl, Die, WFE, FWA, Cab, Utility, 3 Pt, European Box, 5537, NIB $15
Notes:

□ 3140, 1991, Ertl, Die, FWA, Cab, W/Loader, 3 Attachments, 3 Point, 5648EF, NIB $20
Notes:

□ 3350, 1989, Ertl, Die, WFE, FWA, Cab, Utility, Chrome Or Black 3 Pt, Black Grill, Adapts To Britains, 5580EO, NIB $15
□ ALSO SAME, Except No Black Grill, Side Panels, 5580EO, NIB $15
Notes:

□ 3350, 1991, Ertl, Die, FWA, Cab, W/Loader & 3 Attachments, 3 Pt, 5647, NIB $20
Notes:

□ 4020, 2004, Ertl/RC, Die, TBE15609, NA

□ 4430, 1972, Ertl, Die, Cab, NF, High Or Low Hitch, Black Or Yellow Front Wheels, No 66, NIB $20
Notes

□ 4440, 1979, Ertl, Die, Cab, NF, No 66, 1NIB $18
Notes:

□ 4450, 1979, Ertl, Die, Cab, NF, Light Bar Top Front Of Hood, NIB $15
Notes:

□ 4440, 1986, Ertl, Die, Sound-Gard Cab, 66EO, NIB $12
Notes:

□ 4450, 1988, Ertl, Die, NF, Light Bar Top Front Of Hood, NIB $10
Notes:

□ 5410, 2002, Britains For Ertl/RC, Plastic With Metal Chassis, Removable Cab, Steering Front Axle, NIB $20
Notes:

□ 6200, Ertl, Die, With Loader, 5720, NIB $20
Notes:

□ 6410, 1999, Ertl Elite, Die, 00-175, NIB $14
Notes:

☐ **7020, 2004, Ertl/RC, Die, 4WD, TBE15610, NA**
☐ **ALSO SAME, Except "2003 National Farm Toy Show," NA**
Notes:

☐ **7400, 1996, Ertl, Plastic, MFWD, NIB $12**
Notes:

☐ **7410, 2001, Ertl/RC, Plastic, Radio-Controlled, 5204, NIB $18**
Notes:

☐ **7410, 2001, Ertl/RC, Plastic, 5329 MFWD, Plastic, 34507, NIB $10**
Notes:

☐ **7800, 1994, Ertl, Die, Wire Control, 5724DO, NIB $20**
Notes:

☐ **8400, 1995, Ertl, Die, Precision Classic #8, Duals, 5259DO, NIB $90**
Notes:

☐ **8400, 1997, ED, Precision Classic, Duals, New Graphics, 5259CP, NIB $85**
Notes:

☐ **8960, 1989, Ertl, Plastic, WFE, 4WD, Cab, Battery Operated, 3 Pt, PTO, Duals, 5582DO, NIB $35**
Notes:

☐ **9420T, 2002, Ertl/RC, Die, Tracked Tractor, Precision Series II #2, TBE15286, NIB $75**
Notes:

☐ A, 1988, Ertl, Die, On Steel, 5598EO, $5-7
Notes:

Begin 1/43 Scale

☐ A, 1992, SpecCast, Pewter, JDMO14, NIB $15
☐ A, 1996, SpecCast, Die, Painted Pewter, JDMO83, NIB $20
Notes:

☐ A, 1999, Ertl, Die, Unstyled On Steel, 33532, $5-7
Notes:

☐ AR, 1992, SpecCast, Pewter, JDMO19, NIB $18
Notes:

☐ B, 1990, SpecCast, Pewter, JDM002, NIB $15
☐ B, 1995, SpecCast, Pewter, On Steel, Painted Pewter, NIB $20
Notes:

☐ D, 1991, SpecCast, Pewter, JDM004, NIB $18
☐ D, 1994, SpecCast, Pewter, On Steel, JDM052, NIB $18
☐ D, 1995, SpecCast, Pewter, CUST329, NIB $18
Notes:

☐ D, 1991, SpecCast, Pewter, On Steel, "St. Louis Expo," NIB $22
Notes:

☐ The detail on the "St. Louis Expo" pewter tractor from the left can be clearly seen in this close-up photo. Pewter holds impressions well and photographs extremely well, especially for black and white.
Notes:

☐ G, 1992, SpecCast, Pewter, JDM018, NIB $18
Notes:

□ GP, 1991, SpecCast, Pewter, WFE, NIB $17
Notes:

□ GP, 1991, SpecCast, Pewter, JDM010, NIB $17
Notes:

□ GP, 1991, SpecCast, Pewter, Wide Tread, NIB $17
Notes:

□ H, 1992, SpecCast, Pewter, JDM005, NIB $18
Notes:

□ 60, 1990, SpecCast, Pewter, JDM003, NIB $18
Notes:

□ 620, SpecCast, Pewter, JDM-015, NIB $20
□ ALSO SAME, Except 2001, "Grand Opening Moline Tractor & Plow Co," 250 Made, NIB $25
Notes:

□ 630, 1993, SpecCast, Pewter, JDM021, NIB $20
□ 630, 1996, SpecCast, Pewter, Painted Pewter, JDM082, NIB $22
Notes:

□ 630, 1988, Ertl, Die, LP WF, "1988 National Farm Toy Show", 7500 Made, 5599MA, NIB $22
□ ALSO SAME, Except No Inscription, 5599, NIB $8
Notes:

□ 630 LP, 1999, Ertl, Die, WFE, 33533, NIB $8
Notes:

□ 730, 1991, SpecCast, Pewter, JDM-006, NIB $25
Notes:

□ 830, 1991, SpecCast, Pewter, Stock # JDM009, NIB $25
Notes:

□ 4010, 1990, SpecCast, Pewter, JDM001, NIB $20
Notes:

□ 4010, 1993, "1993 National Farm Toy Show," 5725EA, NIB $18
Notes:

□ 4020, 1995, SpecCast, Pewter, ROPS, Canopy, Antique, Engraved Roof, "Expo '96," NIB $22
□ ALSO SAME, Except "Expo '96 Dealer Edition," NIB $22
□ 4020, 1996, SpecCast, Pewter, With ROPS, JDM 085, NIB $22
□ 4020, 1995, SpecCast, Pewter, JDMO72, NIB $22
Notes:

□ 4230, Diesel W/ROPS, 1998 National Show, 5131MA, NIB $25
Notes:

□ 4010, 1993, Ertl, Die, "European Tour," Toy Farmer Edition, NIB $35 *Notes:*

□ 4955, 2002, SpecCast, Pewter, Front Weights, FWD, NIB $30
Notes:

□ 5300, 1992, SpecCast, Pewter, JDM020, NIB $15
Notes:

☐ 5400, 1992, SpecCast, Pewter, WFE, ROPS, Limited Edition 5400 Spirit Tractor Replica, Nashville, NIB $18
Notes:

☐ 8400, 1997, SpecCast, Pewter, Expo 97, Duals, JDM090, NIP $35
Notes:

(Photo Courtesy Of SpecCast)

☐ 8400T, 2000, SpecCast, Pew-ter, JDM141, NIB $28
☐ ALSO SAME, Except With Desk Pen Set, JDM125, NIB $28
Notes:

(Photo Courtesy Of SpecCast)

☐ D, 1930, KT, Lead, Slush Cast, Poor Detail, Rarely Seen, Exc-ellent $400
Notes:

Begin 1/50 Scale

☐ 9300, 2001, SpecCast, Pewter, JDM161, NIP $35
☐ ALSO SAME, Except Part Of Desk Pen Set, NIP $40
Notes:

(Photo Courtesy Of SpecCast)

☐ 9400T, 2002, SpecCast, Pew-ter, JDM120, NIP $28
Notes:

(Photo Courtesy Of SpecCast)

☐ Notice how much detail SpecCast packs into their small toys, in this case the track of their 9400T tractor, made for the first time in 2002.
Notes:

☐ A, 1967, Ertl, Die, Row Crop, Styled, Riveted Wheels With Transmission Breather/Filler, Hitch Hook, 1304, NIP $7
☐ A, 1988, RB, Pewter, NF, Copy Of Ertl, NIP $15
Notes:

Begin 1/64 Scale

☐ A, 1985, ScaMo, Plastic, NF on Steel Or Rubber, Various Colors, With Chrome Label On Top Of Package, Bubble Pack, NIB $8
☐ ALSO SAME, Except No Chrome Label, NIB $8
Notes:

☐ **A, 1995, Ertl, Die, 50th Anniv, Wooden Box, 5305EA, NIP $12**
Notes:

☐ **A, 2000, Ertl, Die, W/Man, Furrow Magazine Card, 15154, NIP $5**
Notes:

☐ **A, Ertl, Die, On Blue Print Card, 1304, NIP $75**
Notes:

☐ **A, 2003, Ertl/RC, Die, Metal Rims, With Man, "Collector Edition 2003," NIP $8**
Notes:

☐ **B, Ertl, Die, NIP $4**
Notes:

☐ **D, Ertl, Die, On Blue Print Card, 1303, NIP $40**
Notes:

☐ **D, 1967, Ertl, Die, WFE, Standard, Wide Seat, W/ Or W/O Drawbar Ext. Detail, Hitch Hook, Part Of Historical Set, 1303, NA**
☐ **ALSO SAME, Except Narrow Seat, Ribbed Wheels, No Hitch Hook, Part Of Historical Set, 1303, NA**
☐ **D, 1988, RB, Pewter, WFE, Copy of Ertl, Antique Tractor, NA**
Notes:

☐ **D, 1999, Ertl, Die, JD Commons Anniversary Model, 15051, NIP $18**
Notes:

☐ **D, 2000, Ertl, Die, On Furrow Magazine Card, 15157, NIP $6**
Notes:

☐ **D, 2000, Ertl, Die, 15136, NIP $4**
Notes:

☐ **G, 1986, ScaMo, NF, Styled, On Rubber, Side-by-Side Stacks, Various Colors NIP $3**
☐ **ALSO SAME, Except Styled, On Steel, NIP $6**
Notes:

☐ **G, 1995, Ertl, Die, On Rubber, From Set 5523ER, NIP $3**
☐ **ALSO SAME, Except 1988, "Steel" Wheels, From Set 5523, NIP $3**
Notes:

☐ **H, NIP $3**
Notes:

☐ **L, Steve Keith, Custom, Green, NIP $40**
Notes:

☐ **M, 1988, Ertl, Die, From 5523 Set, NIP $3**
Notes:

☐ **M, Keith, Custom, NIP $35**
Notes:

☐ **M, Keith, NF, Custom, NIP $35**
Notes:

☐ **R, 1988, Ertl, Die, From 5523 Set, NIP $3**
Notes:

☐ **WA-14, Buehler, Custom, NIB $125**
Notes:

☐ **WA-17, Buehler, Green And Yellow, Custom, NIP $125**
Notes:

☐ **44, 1989, Parts Expo, Nashville, Winning Edge, Dec 1989, NIP $25**
Notes:

☐ **50 Series, 1992, Ertl, Die, WFE, Cab, FWA, Front Weights, With Sound, 5693FO, NIP $6**
Notes:

☐ **50, 1997, Ertl, Die, NF, Shelf Model, 5168, NIP $6**
☐ **50, Ertl, Die, "1998 Iowa FFA Edition," In Fancy Box, 16004A, NIB $15**
Notes:

☐ **55 Series, 1991, Ertl, Die, FWA, New Paint Pattern, 5612FO, NIP $6**
☐ **ALSO SAME, Except Duals, 5806FO, NIP $9**
☐ **ALSO SAME, Except With Loader, 5613FO, NIP $8**
Notes:

☐ **55 Series, 1991, Ertl, Die, FWA, "JD Parts Expo, Phoenix," 5612MA, NIP $20**
Notes:

☐ **60, WF, 2000, 11th In National Museum Series, 16047A, NIP $8**
Notes:

☐ **60, Ertl, Die, On Blue Print Card, 1305, NIP $100**
Notes:

☐ 80, 1995, Ertl, Die, On Rubber, From Set 5523ER, NIP $3
Notes:

☐ 330, 2000, Ertl, Die, On Furrow Magazine Card, 15158, NIP $5
Notes:

☐ 430, 1988, Keith, SC, WFE, Custom, NIP $35
Notes:

☐ 430, 1997, Ertl, Die, Row Crop, 5620EO, Part Of Historical Set, NIP $5
Notes:

☐ 520, 1997, Ertl, Die, WF, Shelf Model, 5193, NIP $4
ALSO SAME, Except "1999 Iowa FFA Edition," Fancy Box, 160-13A, NIP $15
Notes:

☐ 530, WF, Dual On Left Side, 5194, NIP $4
Notes:

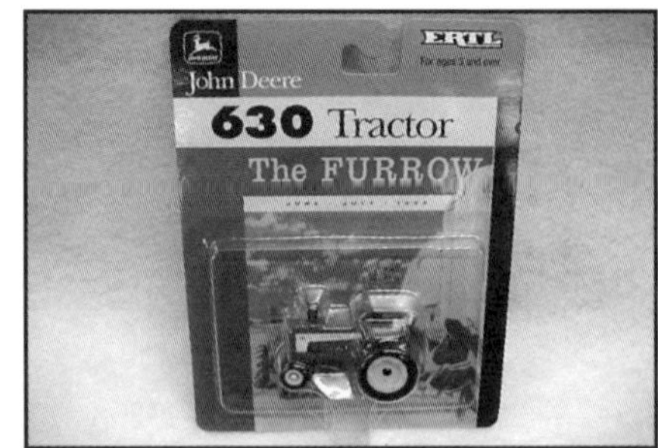

☐ 620, 1999, Ertl, Die, NF, Shelf Model, 5205EO, NIP $6
Notes:

☐ 630, 1995, Ertl, Die, LP, Part Of #4496, (Which Also Includes a Ford 9N, Allis-Chalmers WD, IH 966, Massey-Ferguson 3140, Caterpillar Challenger 45), Ertl 50th Anniversary, NA
Notes:

☐ 630, 2000, Ertl, Die, NF, Furrow Mag Replica Card, 15153, NIP $6
☐ ALSO SAME, Except WF, $6
Notes:

☐ 630, 1985, Baker, Row Crop, Represents 1958-1960 Model, NIP $30
Notes:

☐ 730, 1967, Ertl, Die, RC, Metal Fenders, Riveted Rear Axles, W/ W/O Hitch Hook, Part Of Historical Set, 1006, NIP $125
☐ ALSO SAME, But 1969, Plas Fenders, 730 Decals, Riveted Or Stamped Rear Axles, W/W/O Hitch Hook, Hist. Set, 1306, NIP $75
☐ ALSO SAME, Except 1988, RB, Pewter, Copy of Ertl, $15

☐ 730, 1988, Keith, SC, NF Or WFE, Custom, NIP $35
☐ ALSO SAME, Except "1988 Lafayette Show," Custom, NIP $40
Notes:
,

☐ 730, Ertl, Die, Blue Print Card, W/Numbers, Shelf, 1306, NIP $100
☐ ALSO SAME, Except Without Numbers, NIP $70
Notes:

☐ 820, WF, On Card, 15137, NIP $5
Notes:

☐ 830, 1987, Keith, SC, WFE, Custom, NIP $40
Notes:

☐ 2510, 1996, Ertl, Die, NF, Shelf Model, 5756, NIP $5
Notes:

☐ 4010, 1970, Ertl, Die, Metal Fenders, On Blue Print Card, Shelf Model, 1307, NIP $100
☐ ALSO SAME, Except Plastic Fenders, NIP $60
☐ ALSO SAME, Except 1988, RB, Pewter, Copy of Ertl, NIP $20
Notes:

☐ 4020, C&D, NF, Custom, NIP $25
Notes:

☐ **4020, 1989, Keith/Matsen, SC, NF Or WFE, Cabs Or Duals, NIP $30**
☐ **ALSO SAME, Except LPG, Custom, NIP $30**
☐ **ALSO SAME, Except Wheatland, NIP $25**
Notes:

☐ **4020, WF, HO Scale, 33550, NIP $5**
Notes:

☐ **4020, 1998, Ertl, Die, HO Scale, 5460CO, NIP $6**
Notes:

☐ **4020, 2001, Ertl/RC, Die, FWA, Cab, TBE15218, NIP $6** *Notes:*

☐ **4230, 1972, Ertl, Die, Blue Print Card, Small Narrow Front Wheels, Shelf, 1308, NIP $125**
☐ **ALSO SAME, Except 1974, Gold Plated, Dealer Award, Some On Plaque, 1619, NIP $150**
Notes:

☐ **4230, 1972, Ertl, Die, Blue Print Card, Large Wheels, Regular Decal, Shelf, 1308, NIP $75**
Notes:

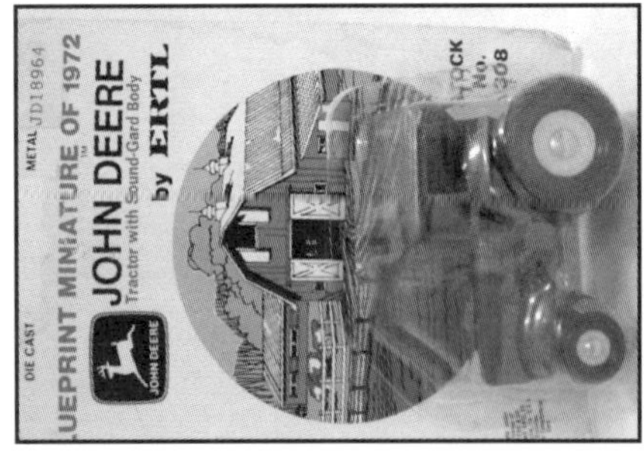

☐ **4230, 1972, Ertl, Die, Blue Print Card, Large Wheels, No Decal, Shelf, 1308, NIP $85**
Notes:

☐ **4320, 1986, Gunning, SC, WFE, 5 Varieties, NIP $30**
Notes:

☐ **4430, 1979, Ertl, Die, Metal Stack, Yellow Decal, Shelf, 1619, NIP $35**
Notes:

☐ 4430, Ertl, Die, No Muffler, Yellow Decal, Narrow Wheels, Box, 519, NIP $125
☐ 4430, Ertl, Die, WFE, Cab, Gold-Plated Ertl Employee Award, NIP $180
Notes:

☐ 4430, Ertl, Die, European Card, 1703, Rare, NIP $75
Notes:

☐ 4440, 1983, Ertl, Die, Plastic Stack, Strobe Decals, 1619, NIP $12
☐ ALSO SAME, Except 1980, Metal Stack, NIP $20
Notes:

☐ 4440, 2 Plastic Stacks, Yellow Strobe, No Front Weights, 1619, NIP $12
Notes:

☐ 4450, 1983, Ertl, Die, Metal Stack, Silver Decal, Shelf, 5509FO, NIP $6
Notes:

☐ 4450, 1984, Ertl, Same As Model Listed At Left, With Front Weights, 5509, NIP $8
Notes:

☐ 4450, 1985, POW-R-PULL, Motorized, With Muffler Cap, 4092, NIP $15
Notes:

☐ 4450, 1986, Ertl, Die, MFD, Shelf Model, 5517, NIP $6
Notes:

☐ 4450, 1986, Ertl, Die, Duals, Front Weights, 5516, NIP $12
☐ ALSO SAME, Except No Front Weights, Shelf Model, 5516, NIP $6
Notes:

☐ 4450, 1986, Ertl, Die, With Loader, Shelf Model, 587, NIP $6
☐ ALSO SAME, Except No Loader And No Muffler Cap, 4092, NIP $6
Notes:

☐ 4450, 1986, Ertl, Die, 2 Plastic Stacks, Silver Front Decal, No Front Weights, 5509, NIP $8
☐ 4450, 1986, Ertl, Die, Metal Muffler, Silver Front Decal, No Front Weights, 5509, NIP $15
Notes:

☐ 4450, Front Weights, With Loader Bracket, 5509, NIP $6
☐ ALSO SAME, Except No Loader Bracket, 5509, NIP $13
☐ ALSO SAME, Except 1992, Ertl, Die, WFE, Cab, "The Winning Edge, Nashville Parts Expo" 5509MA, NIP $30
Notes:

☐ 4455, 1989, Ertl, Die, 2WD, Shelf Model, 5571, NIP $5
☐ ALSO MANY VARIETIES, 1989 Or 1990, With Or Without MFD, Duals, Loader, 560, 5612, 5613, All NIP $5
☐ ALSO SAME, Except 1990, "Phoenix Parts Expo," 5612MA, NIP $5
Notes:

☐ 4520, 2002, Ertl/RC, Die, With Hiniker Cab, NF, Duals, TBE-15438, NIP $7
Notes:

☐ 4620, C&D, Cab, Custom, NIP $40
Notes:

☐ 4650, With Loader Brackets, NA
Notes:

☐ 5010, 1999, Ert, Die, Replica Collector Edition, 2400 Made, 16018A, NIP $20
Notes:

☐ 5010, WF, On Card, 15138, NIP $6
Notes:

□ 5020, 1989, ScaMo, Plastic, WFE, Standard, Kinze Conversion, V-8, "Louisville 2-15-89," Kinze Decal, Blue Or Green, NIP $12
Notes:

□ 5020, 1989, ScaMo, Plastic, WFE, Standard, Kinze Conversion, V-8, Green, NIP $5
Notes:

□ 5020, 1997, Ertl, Die, Natl Farm Toy Museum, "NFTM" On Fenders, 3051MA, NIP $6
5020, 1997, Ertl, Die, "8th National Farm Toy Show" Series, 7500 Made, 3061MA, , NIP $7
Notes:

□ 5020, 1997, Ertl, Die, 5776FO, NIP $6
Notes:

□ 5020, 2000, Ertl, Die, On Furrow Magazine Card, 15155, NIP $6
Notes:

□ 6030, C&D, Cab, Duals, Custom, NIP $35
Notes:

□ 6200, With Duals And ROPS, 5734, NIP $4
□ ALSO SAME, Except 1994, NO ROPS, NIP $4
□ ALSO SAME, Except 2WD, Shelf Model, 5733, NIP $4
□ ALSO SAME, Except RC And ROPS, 5733, NIP $4
Notes:

□ 6210, 1998, Ertl, Die, MFD, Shelf Model, 5170, NIP $10
Notes:

□ 6400, 1996, Ertl, Die, With Revised Loader, Shelf, 5929EO, NIP $6
Notes:

□ 6400, With FWA And ROPS, 5729, NIP $6
□ ALSO SAME, Except MFWD, 5729, NIP $6
□ 6400, 1996, Ertl, Die, Duals, MFWD, "People Make The Difference" On Top Of Hood, "JD Aftermarket 2000," NIP $15
Notes:

□ 6410, 1998, Ertl, Die, With Loader, Shelf Model, 5169, NIP $6
Notes:

□ 6420, 2002, Ertl/RC, Die, FWA, "1st Production" Stamped On Bottom, 15226, NIP $6
□ ALSO SAME, But No Stamp, TBE40545, NIP $5
Notes:

□ 7020, 1989, Baker, Sandcast, 4WD, "Gateway St. Louis" Show, NIP $100
Notes:

□ 7020, 2004, Ertl/RC, Die, Vintage 4WD, Articulated, Single Rubber Tires, NIP $6
Notes:

□ 7520, Baker, Custom, 1998, 4WD, No AC, 1998 Show, RLB10, NIP $75
Notes:

□ 7520, C&D, Custom, Triples, NIP $65
Notes:

□ 7600, 1994, Ertl, Die, Motorized, Shelf Model, 5672, NIP $6
□ ALSO SAME, Except MFWD, With Sound, D5750EO, NIP $10
Notes

□ 7610, 1999, Ertl, Die, Motorized, Shelf Model, 5203, NIP $6
Notes:

☐ 7710, 2001, Ertl/RC, Die, FWA, Duals, TBE15316, NIP $5
Notes:

☐ 7800, 1992, Ertl, Die, MFD, 5651FO, NIP $4
☐ ALSO SAME Except Duals, NIP $9
☐ ALSO SAME, Except "'93 Parts Expo Servicegard," 5651MA, NIP $25
☐ ALSO SAME, Except "1994 Farm Festival," Fancy Box, NIP $12
☐ ALSO SAME, Except "Minnesota State Fair," NIP $15
Notes:

☐ 7800, 1992, Ertl, Die, MFD, With Loader, 5652FO, $8
Notes:

☐ 7800, 1993, Ertl,, Die, 2WD, No Roof Decal, Green & White JD Card, 5538FO, NIP $6
☐ ALSO SAME, Except Blue Farm Machines Card, 5538FP, NIP $6
☐ ALSO SAME, Except "Customer Roundup Parts Expo" Decal On Cab Roof, 5538MA, NIP $30
Notes:

☐ 7800, 1995, Ertl, Die, Duals, "St Louis Parts Expo," WFE, 5649NA, NIP $25
Notes:

☐ 7800, 2000, Ertl, Die, "Achieving The Vision, JD Aftermarket 2000 St. Louis," Decal On Cab Roof, 5649NA, NIP $20
Notes:

☐ 7810, 1996, Ertl, Die, MFD, Shelf Model, 5202FO, NIP $12
Notes:

☐ 8010, Steve Keith, Articulated, NIP $150
Notes:

☐ 8010, Steve Keith, Articulated, With Cab, NIP $150
Notes:

□ 8020, 2004, Ertl/RC, Die, Vintage 4WD, TBE15616, NA
Notes:

□ 8020, C& D, Diesel With Duals, Cab, Articulated, NIP $150
Notes:

□ 8020, C& D, Diesel With Duals, Cab, Articulated, NIP $150
Notes:

□ 8100, 1997, Ertl, Die, MFWD, "Mission, John Deere-San Antonio 1997," 5065MA, NIP $30
Notes:

□ 8100, 1997, Ertl, Die, MFWD, TBE5065, NIP $6
Notes:

□ 8200, 1997, Ertl, Die, 2WD, With Flotation Front Tires, 5064EO, NIP $6
Notes:

□ 8210, 1999, Ertl, Die, 2WD, Shelf Model, 15064, NIP $4
□ ALSO SAME, Except With Flotation Front Tires, 15064, NIP $4
Notes:

□ 8220, 2003, Ertl/RC, Die, Wide Tires, TBE15496, NIP $6
Notes:

□ 8300, 1996, Ertl, Die, MFD, Shelf Model, 5063FO, NIP $6
Notes:

□ 8310, 1999 Nashville Dealer Meeting, NIP $25
Notes:

□ 8310T, 1998, Ertl, Die, NA
□ ALSO SAME, Except "John Deere Kansas City," 5080MA, NIP $45
□ ALSO SAME, Except "JD Director Conference--Experience 300T, 1998," 5080MA, NIP $45
Notes:

□ 8400, 1996, Ertl, Die, With FWA & Duals, 5927FO, NIP $6
Notes:

□ 8400T, 1997, Ertl, Die, Shelf Model, 5051EO, NIP $7
□ ALSO SAME, Except 1998, "1998 Ertl Collectors' Conference," Very Limited, NIP $100
Notes:

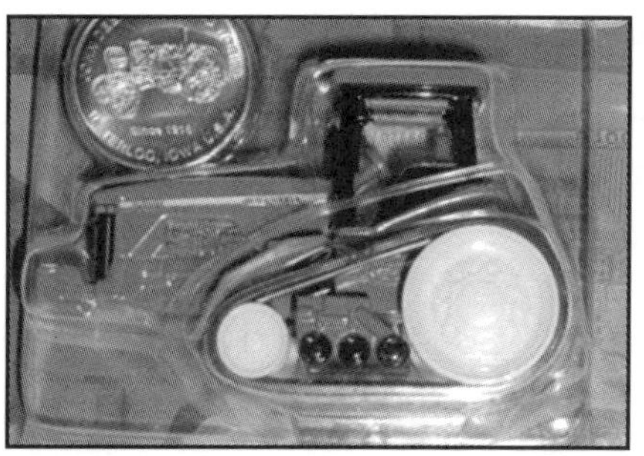

□ 8400T, Medal, Fancy Card, Waterloo Works, 5000 Made, 5195, NIP $30
Notes:

□ 8410, 1999, Ertl, Die, FWA, 15065, NIP $6
□ ALSO SAME, With FWA And Duals, 15062, NIP $4
□ ALSO SAME, Except 2000, MFD, Triples, "'99 Farm Progress Show," 15118A, NIP $20
Notes:

□ 8410T, Ertl, Die, With Book, "Book Buddies," 36666, NIP $6
Notes:

□ 8410T, 2000, Ertl, Die, Tracked, TBE15100, NIP $7
Notes:

□ 8420, 2002, Ertl/RC, Die And Plastic, Duals, Plastic Front Axle, 15413, NIP $3
Notes:

☐ 8420, 2001, Ert/RC, Die, With Front And Rear Duals, TBE15225, NIP $7
Notes:

☐ 8420, 2002, Ertl/RC, Die, European Tractor, TBE15409, NIP $7
Notes:

☐ 8430, Darrell J Baker, Kit, NIP $45
Notes:

☐ 8440, Baker, Custom, 4WD, NIP $50
Notes:

☐ 8520T, 2002, Ertl/RC, Die, TBE-15224, NIP $7
Notes:

☐ 8630, 1994, Baker, Spincast, 13th Mid-America Gateway Toy Show, NIP $55
Notes:

☐ 8640, Baker, 4WD, Kit, Custom, NIP $45
Notes:

☐ 8560, 1993, Ertl, Die, 4WD, Shelf, Exactly Like 8760 Except For Decal, 5603, NIP $15
Notes:

☐ 8760, 1993, Ertl, Die, 4WD, Shelf Model, 5603EP, NIP $12
Notes:

□ 8850, 1983, Ertl, Die, 4WD, Shelf, 575, NIP $25
□ ALSO SAME, Except Light Green (Also Called "Wrong Green",) NIP $35
□ ALSO SAME, Except "Heart Of America Show," 1260 Made, 575KC, NIP $40
Notes:

□ 8850, 1986, Ertl, Die, 4WD, Friction Motor, Shelf Model, 551EO, NIP $11
Notes:

□ 8870, 1994, Ertl, Die, 4WD, 5791, NIP $14
Notes:

□ 8870, 2002, Ertl, Die, Revised Edition, Wider Duals, Updated Rims, Articulated, 15322, NA
Notes:

□ 9320, 2002, Ertl/Die, 4WD Tractor D-Kit, TBE15429, NIP $7
Notes:

□ 9400, 2000, Ertl, Die, Triples, Shelf Model, 5937EO, NIP $7
□ ALSO SAME, Except Duals, 15321, NIP $7
□ ALSO SAME, Except 3 Point Hitch, Lights, Handrail, "99 Expo, KFYR," NIP $50
Notes:

□ 9400, 2001, Ertl/RC, Die, 4WD Kit, TBE15294, NIP $7
Notes:

□ 9400T, 2000, Ertl, Die, TBE-15015, NIP $8
Notes:

□ 9420, 2002, Ertl, Die, Triples All Around, 15222, NIP $8
Notes:

□ **9420T, 2002, Ertl, Die, 15223, NIP $8**
Notes:

□ **9620, 2004, Ertl/RC, Die, Wide Single Tires, Articulated, 4WD, TBE15678, NIP $7**
Notes:

□ **9620T, 2004, Ertl/RC, Die, Tracked Tractor, Free-Rolling Rubber Tracks, TBE15679, NIP $7**
Notes:

□ **8410, 2000, Ertl, Die, 15065, 1/87 Scale, NIP $5**
Notes:

Begin 1/87 Scale

□ **Dain, 2000, ScaMo, Die, FY-0029, 1/16 Scale, NIB $65**
Notes:

Begin Dain

□ **Froelich, 1985, ScaMo, SCA, No 7 In JLE Threshers Series, 1/16 scale, NIB $80**
Notes:

Begin Froelich In Various Scales

□ **Froelich, 1993, SpecCast, Pewter, JDM024, 1/16 Scale, NIB $22**
□ **ALSO SAME, Except "1993 Nashville Aftermarket Conference," Antique Brass, Stock No JDM025, NIB $25**
Notes:

□ **Froelich, Ertl, Die, 1/64 On Blue Print Card, Shelf Model, 1301, NIP $50**
Notes:

□ **Waterloo Boy, 1973, Cox, SCA, Model R, WFE, On Steel, Only Made 19, 1/16 Scale, NIB $800**
Notes:

Begin Waterloo Boy In Various Scales

□ Waterloo Boy, 1981, SM, SCA, #3 In JLE Series, 1/16 Scale, $25-35
Notes:

□ Waterloo Boy, 1988, Ertl, Die, Model R, Collector Insert, Special Edition, Special Drawbar Hitch, 1/16 Scale, 559DA $30-40
ALSO SAME, Except Shelf Model, Normal Radiator, 559DO, $20-25
Notes:

Waterloo Boy, 2000, Ertl, Die, Precision Classics, 1/16 Scale, 150-13, NIP $95
Notes:

□ Waterloo Boy, 1990, SpecCast, Pewter, WFE, On Steel, 1990 JD Parts Expo, JDM-007, 1/43 Scale, NIB $18
□ ALSO SAME, Except, 1991, Brass Radiator, JDM-008, 1/43 Scale, NIB $25
Notes:

□ Overtime, 1990, Ertl, Die, "1990 Special Edition," 1/32 Scale, 5607, $5-8
Notes:

□ Waterloo Boy, 2004, Ertl/RC, Die, Free-Rolling Metal Wheels, 1/32, TBE15613, NIB $14
Notes:

□ Waterloo Boy, 1967, Ertl, Die, Short Fan Shaft, Long Transmission Breather, Hitch Hook, Ribbed Or Smooth Wheels, 1302, 1/64 Scale, NIP $4
□ ALSO SAME, Except Short Transmission Breather, No Hitch Hook, NIP $4
Notes:

□ Waterloo Boy, 1988, Ertl, Die, Red Transmission Breather, Part Of 5523 Set, 1/64, Scale, NIP $4
□ Waterloo Boy, 1988, RB, Pewter, WFE, Antique Tractor, Copy Of Ertl, 1/64 Scale, NIP $18
Notes:

□ Waterloo Boy, Ertl, Die, Blue Print Card, Shelf Model, 1/64 Scale, 1302, $49-50
Notes:

☐ A, 1949, Eska, SCA, 34," NF, Open Grill, Open Engine, Rare, $4000
Notes:

☐ A, 1999, Ertl, Die, 38," Pedal, NF, Reissue, 15035, NIB $125
Notes:

☐ Loader, Ertl, Plastic And Metal, For 7000 Or 8000 Series Pedal Tractor With WFE, Green Or Black, 12159G, NIB $65
Notes:

☐ Trailer, 1962, Ertl, PS, Trailer, 2 Wheel, No Fenders, Metal Rims, 535, Excellent-NIB $85-150
☐ ALSO SAME, Except 1970, Plastic Rims 5350AO, Excellent-NIB $35-50
Notes:

☐ 10, 1961, Ertl, SCA, 37," Pedal, NF, 3 Holes In Engine, $650
☐ 10, 1961, Eska, SCA, 37," Pedal, NF, 4 Holes In Engine, $700
Notes:

☐ 10, 1992, Riecke, SC, NF, Model of Pedal Tractor, 1/16 Scale, $45
Notes:

☐ 10, 1997, Ertl, Die, NF, 3 Holes, 6 3/8" Long X 3 3/8" Wide X 4 1/4" High, 1st In Series III "National Farm Toy Museum," 1/8 Scale, NIB $40
Notes:

☐ 20, 1963, Ertl, SCA, 38," Pedal, NF, No Holes, PTO Lever, 532, Excellent-NIB $300-600
☐ 20, 1965, Ertl, SCA, 38," NF, Holes, PTO Lever, 532, Excellent $300
Notes:

☐ 30, 1973, Ertl, SCA, 37," NF, 2 Variations, 520, Excellent-NIB $150-400
Notes:

□ 40, 1978, Ertl, SCA, 37," NF, 520, Excellent-NIB $150-400
□ 50, 1982, Ertl, SCA, 37," NF, Same As "40," Except Decal, 520, Excellent-NIB $150-400
Notes:

□ 50, 1985, Ertl, SCA, 37," NF, Different Casting, 520AO, Excellent-NIB $150-375
Notes:

□ 55, 1990, Ertl, Die, NF, Industrial, Yellow, Excellent-NIB $300-500
Notes:

□ 60, 1954, Eska, SCA, 34," NF, Small Version, Muffler, 5 Variations, Excellent $675
□ ALSO SAME, Except 38", Large Version, 2 Variations, Excellent $700
Notes:

□ 130, 1958, Eska, Two-Hole Type, Excellent-NIB $450-700
□ 130, 1959, Eska, Large-Hole Type, Excellent-NIB $450-700
□ 130, Eska, Small-Hole Type, Never Seen NIB, Excellent $800
Notes:

□ 140, 1970, Ertl, SCA, 355," Lawn & Garden, WFE, 531, Excellent-NIB $350-750
Notes:

□ 620, 1956, Eska, SCA, 38," Excellent $700
Notes:

□ 620, Riecke, Custom, 1/16 Scale, NIB $40
Notes:

□ 3140, Rolly, Plastic, Not Marketed In USA, NIB $250
Notes:

□ 4020, 1991, Ertl, Die, WFE, 5682, Excellent-NIB $275-350
Notes:

□ 4300, 2002, Ertl/RC, Plastic, JD Kids' Line, 34380, NA
Notes:

□ 6400, Germany, With Loader, WFE, NIB $200
Notes:

□ 6410, 1999, Rolly Toy, Plastic, WFE, 5099AO, NIB $140
□ ALSO With Loader, 15049, NIB $165
Notes:

□ 7410, 1997, Ertl, Die, WFE, 5828EO, Excellent-NIB $140-165
Notes:

□ 7600, 1994, Ertl, Die, WFE, 552AO, Excellent-NIB $150-200
Notes:

□ 8310, 2000, Ertl, Die, With MFWD, TBE15067, NIB $150
Notes:

□ 8400, 1999, Ertl, Die, WFE, 5099AO, NIB $150
Notes:

□ 8520, 2002, Ertl, Die, MFWD Pedal Tractor With 2-1/2" Wide Rear Tires, 15392, NIB $150
Notes:

☐ Anhydrous Ammonia Tank, 1999, Re-issue, 15010, NIB $18
☐ ALSO SAME, Except 1990, Ertl, Die, 5636DO, Excell-NIB $15-25
Notes:

☐ Baler, 1952, Carter, PS, 14-T With Metal Teeth, 3 Vars Of Hitches, Excellent-NIB $165-325
☐ Baler, 1958, Carter, PS, 14-T Style With Plastic Teeth, Side Hitch, Excellent-NIB $195-400
Notes:

☐ Baler, 1966, ED, 24T, Yellow Pickup & Thrower, Bubble Or Closed Box, 545, Excellent-NIB $50-125
Notes:

☐ Baler, 1974, Ertl, Die, Model 336, 585EO, Excellent-NIB $20-35
☐ ALSO SAME, Except Black Hitch, 585EO, Excellent-NIB $30-45
Notes:

☐ Baler, 1984, Ertl, Die, Round Baler, Clevis Hitch, With Large Yellow Round Bale, 592DO, NIB $25
Notes:

☐ Baler, 1993, Ertl, Die, Green Pickup & Thrower, 585DO, NIB $25
Notes:

☐ Baler, 1994, Riecke, Custom, 14-T, Excellent, $325
Notes:

☐ Baler, 1994, Ertl, Die, 348, Square, 5639, NIB $12
☐ ALSO SAME, Except 1997, New Graphics, 5639YI, NIB $22
Notes:

☐ Baler, 1997, Ertl, Die, 214-T, Precision Classics #11, 5770CO, NIB $90
Notes:

□ Baler, 1999, Ertl, Die, 566, Round, 5819, NIB $22
Notes:

□ Baler, 2001, Ertl, Die, 567, Round, Rear Door Opens, One Plastic Round Bale, 15176, NIB $22
Notes:

□ Baler, 1995, Ertl, Die, Square, 5911DO, NIB $25
Notes

□ Bales, 2002, Ertl, Plastic, Light Green, 13189, NA
Notes:

□ Ertl's Precision Baler, 5770CO, was first made in 1995, and the many details are what make the toy so interesting.
Notes:

□ Combine, 1930, Vindex, CI, Pull Type, Silver, With Standing Man, Scarce, Excellent $4500
Notes:

□ Combine, 1952, Carter, PS, 12A, Pull Type, With Canvas, Varied Levers & Spring Clips, No Box #, Excellent-NIB $175-350
Notes:

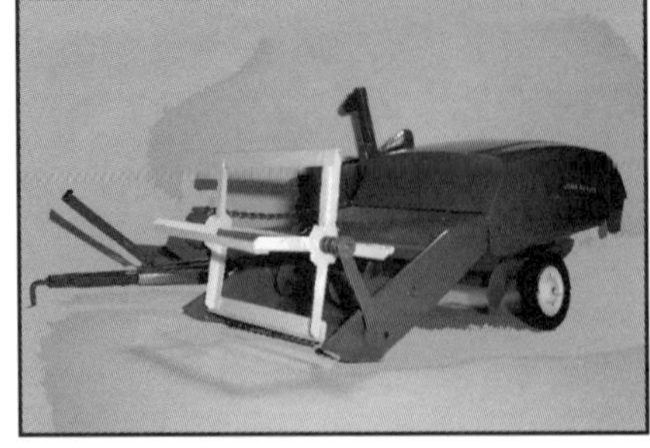

□ Combine, 1956 Carter, PS, 30, Pull Type, With Auger In Header No Box #, Excellent-NIB $400-1000
Notes:

□ Combine, 1990, Weber, Custom, Model 30, Very Detailed, Very Limited Production, NA
Notes:

☐ **D, 1994, Ertl, Die, "100th Anniversary Minnesota Division 1994" (Around Outside Of Flywheel), Gold Paint, 5718, NIB $185**
Notes:

☐ **Waterloo Boy, 1994, Ertl, Die, British Overtime Model, 5811DO, NIB $22**
Notes:

☐ **A, 1995, Ertl, Die, "125th Anniversary Kansas City Branch," Gold-Plated, 5046PA, NIB $165**
Notes:

☐ **730, 1988, Yoder, Plastic, Red Model NF Or WFE, 225 Made, NIB $100**
Notes:

☐ **420, 1992, Nolt, Custom, Utility Tractor, 3 Pt, Serial Numbered, NIB $265**
Notes:

☐ **AO, 1995, Stephan, Custom, Orchard, 500 Made, NIB $265**
Notes:

☐ **Dain, 1982, Hansen, PS, 1000 Made, NIB $500**
Notes:

☐ **Set, 2004, Ertl/RC, Die, 4240 Tractor With Cab, 535 Round Baler, Rear Door On Baler Opens, Six Plastic Straw Bales, TBE15620, NIB $10**
Notes:

☐ **Wagner WA-17, Clements, Millenium Edition, NIB $700**
Notes:

☐ Spreader, 1930, Vindex, CI, Red, Manure, 4 Wheels, Horse-Drawn, Excellent $3500
Notes:

☐ Baler, 1990, Weber, Custom, Side Discharge Baler, Excellent Detail, NA
Notes:

☐ 140, 1969, Ertl, Die, Individual Tractor Of Set, Patio Red, Decal And Other Variations, 574, Excellent-NIB $225-400
Notes:

☐ A, 1949, Eska, SCA, 34," NF, Open Grill, "Coffin" Engine, Red, Very Rare, $7500
Notes:

☐ Grain Drill, 1991, Ertl, Die, 452, 580DO, NIB $18
Notes:

☐ Engine, 1992, Ertl, Die, Waterloo Boy, "Nashville Parts Expo 1992," 1/8 Scale, 5645, NIB $12
☐ ALSO SAME, Except Shelf Model, Excellent-NIB $10-15
Notes:

☐ Froelich, 2000, Ertl, Die, 1/16 Scale, 15008, Millennium, NIB $45
Notes:

☐ 430, 1988, Trumm, Plastic, Green, Excellent-NIB $35-40
☐ ALSO SAME, Except Yellow, Excellent-NIB $35-40
Notes:

☐ Combine, 1990, Weber, Custom, Model 5A Pull-Type, Very Detailed, Very Limited Production, Custom, NA
Notes:

☐ **GP, 1994, Ertl, Die, Wide Tread, "2-Cylinder Club Expo IV," 5706YA, Excellent-NIB $40-55**
☐ **ALSO, SAME Except Exhibitor's Mdl, 5706, Exc-NIB $60-75**
Notes:

☐ **730, 1995, Yoder, Plastic, Nebraska Dept Of Roads, Only 500 Made, NIB $90**
Notes:

☐ **LA, 1994, SpecCast, Great American Toy Show, Gold Plated, NIB $250**
Notes:

☐ **Lindeman, 1988, Riecke, Custom, Crawler, NIB $300**
Notes:

☐ **Log Skidder, 1975, Ertl, Die, 740, ROPS, 590, Ex-NIB $125-200**
Notes:

☐ **MI, 1990, Ertl, Die, Industrial Tractor, Orange, With Fenders, 5628DO, Excellent-NIB $20-25**
Notes:

☐ **630, 1960, Ertl, Die, Red IH Rear Wheels, NF, Rare, Excellent $800**
Notes:

☐ **4230, Ertl, Die, "21st National Farm Toy Show," Gold, $1,000**
Notes:

☐ **5020, 1969, Ertl, Die, Gold-Plated, $750**
Notes:

☐ 630, 1959, Ertl, Die, Toy Farmer, Gold Plated, NF, 3 Point, Scarce, Excellent $650 *Notes:*

☐ 20, 1997, Die, 1/8 Scale, Yellow Seat, 5917EO, NIB $25
☐ ALSO SAME, Except Yellow Steering Wheel, NIB $25
Notes:

☐ 3650, 1991, Ertl, PL, 40," WFE, FWA, With Loader, (1986-1991 Varieties,) 5675, Excellent-NIB $300-400
Notes:

☐ 110, 1965, Ertl, Die, Half Yellow Seat, 538, Excellent-NIB $75-225
Notes:

☐ 4960 Gold, NIB $400
Notes:

☐ Waterloo Boy, 2000, Rouch, Brass, Custom, NIB $300
Notes:

☐ Set, 2004, Ertl/RC, Die, 6220 Tractor With Wing Mower, DOT Orange, 1/64, TBE15632, NA
Notes:

☐ Skid Steer Loader, 1977, Ertl, Die, Green And Black, Yellow Or White Rims 569, NIB $20
☐ ALSO SAME, Except Green, 569, NIB $20
Notes:

☐ D, 1998, ScaMo, CI, Repro Of Vindex, NIB $110
Notes:

☐ **Corn Picker, 1999, Ertl, Die, 237, Precision Series #14, With 4020, 5083KO, NIB $165**
Notes:

☐ **BI, 1997, Ertl, Die, Tractor, Revision Of BR, Yellow, 5730DO, NIB $25**
Notes:

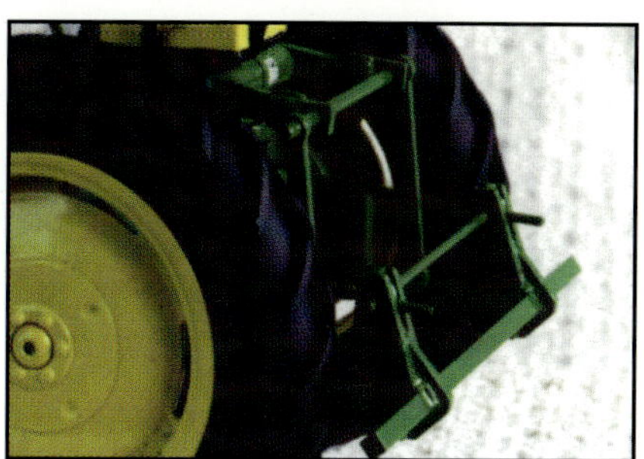

☐ **Tool Bar, 2002, Nolt, Adaptor, Converts 3-Point To Tool Bar, Custom, NA**
Notes:

☐ **40, 1954, Ertl, Die, Crawler, Yellow, Some Came With Green Blade, As Above, Excellent-NIB $300-700**
Notes:

☐ **JD-Lanz, 1963, Lesney, Die, Model 700, WFE, Utility, Gray Tires, 50B, Or Black Tires, Stock No 50, NIB $35**
Notes:

☐ **Grader, 2003, Ertl/RC, Die, 772CH Road, Updated Graphics, 1/50, TBE15527, NA**
Notes:

☐ **3020, Ertl, Die, Gold, Rare, Usually Has Fenders And Muffler, NA**
Notes:

☐ **A, 1985, Ertl, Die, 40th Anniversary, With Driver, Gold, Rare, NIB $400**
Notes:

☐ **Disc, Ertl, Die, 220, Gold Plated, Rare, NIB $400**
Notes:

□ 140, Ertl, Die, Lawn & Garden Tractor, 1/16 Scale, Gold-Plated, Rare, NIB $325
Notes:

□ 140, 1967, Ertl, Die, Lawn & Garden, 1/16 Scale, Plastic Steering Wheel, Other Variations, 550, Excellent-NIB $70-125
Notes:

□ Wheel Loader, 1971, Ertl, Die, 644, Gold Plated, Rare, 1/25 Scale, 503, NIB $400
□ ALSO SAME, Except Regular, With Or Without ROPS, 503, Excellent-NIB $60-85
Notes:

□ 5010, 1999, Ert, Die, Gold Toned, With Commemorative Coin, *Replica* Magazine's 100th Issue Commemorative, 100 Made, 1/64 Scale, 16018A, NIB $450
□ ALSO SAME, Except Green, 2400 Made, 16018A, NIB $20
Notes:

□ A, 1995, Ertl, Die, Gold, "50th Anniversary 1934-1984," NIB $200
Notes:

□ 4520, 2002, Ertl/RC, Die, With Hiniker Cab, WFE, Gold-Plated, NA
Notes:

□ LA, 2002, SpecCast, Die, " 1/16, JDM 173 (No. 3 in series), NIB $35
Notes:

□ 40, 2004, Ertl/RC, Die, Wide Front, Steerable, Rubber Tires, 1/16, TBE15600, NIB $25
Notes:

□ 720, 2004, Ertl/RC, Die, With Blade, Steerable, Blade Swivels, 3-Point Fast Hitch, TBE15601, NIB $30
Notes:

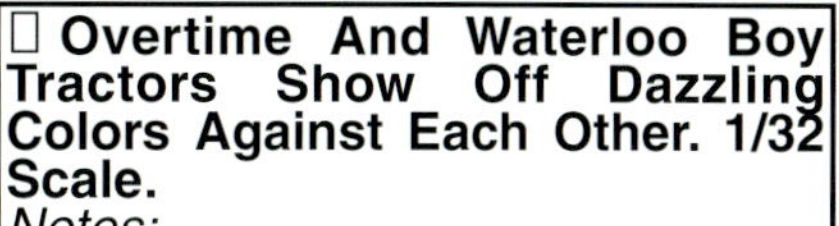

☐ **Overtime And Waterloo Boy Tractors Show Off Dazzling Colors Against Each Other. 1/32 Scale.**
Notes:

☐ **Gold John Deere racing car, still wrapped in its original plastic, comes with "97" on the door.**
Notes:

☐ **The Vindex cardboard dealer display is very rare and very valuable, and shows off the Vindex cast-iron vehicles to their best effect. It was used as a sales tool at implement dealers. The actual display goes only from the bottom of the lower shelf on down.**
Notes:

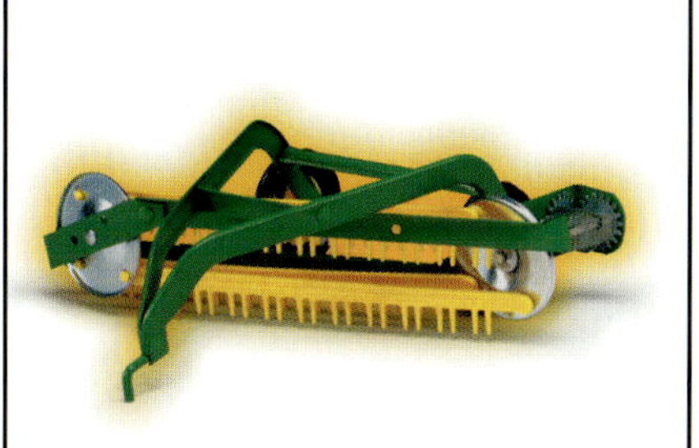

☐ **Rake, 2003, Ertl/RC, Die, Hay, 1/16, TBE15484, NA**
Notes:

☐ **6410, 2002, Ertl/RC, Plastic, With Loader, 9", TBEK15424, NA**
Notes:

☐ **Pickup Advertising 20 Series Tractors, "Power Sizes And Types To Meet Every Farming Need," #113 In Series, 15091, NIB $18**
Notes:

☐ **John Deere boxes can be very colorful, like this one for the Ertl-made John Deere D, NIB $25.**
Notes:

☐ **Engine, 1930, Vindex, Cast Iron, Stationary Gas Engine On Cart, 1/16 Scale, Excellent $800**
Notes:

☐ **6400, 1994, Ertl, Die, With Loader, 5732, 1/64 Scale, NIB $6**
Notes:

☐ 1960, Ertl, Die, Dealer Display, 7 Pieces, Plexiglas Cover, $800
Notes:

☐ 1974, Ertl, Die, Historical Set, 8 Pieces In Shadow Box, 1375, NIB $250
☐ ALSO SAME, Except On Card, 1370, NIB $150
Notes:

☐ 830, 1983, Trumm, CA, Custom, NIB $100
Notes:

☐ 1931 Hawkeye Truck, 1994, Ertl, Die, With Model R Waterloo Boy, 1/32 Scale, 5768DO Excellent-NIB $12-20
Notes:

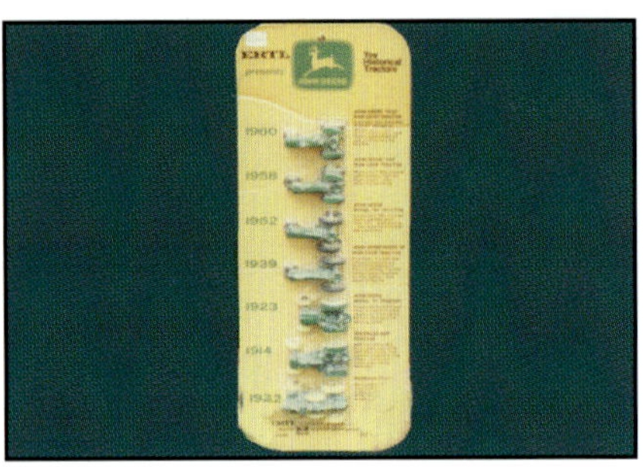

☐ 1960, Ertl, Die, Historical Set, 7 Tractors On Vertical Gold Card, NIP $200
Notes:

☐ X485, 2004, Ertl/RC, L&G Tractor And Attachments, 1/32, TBE-15691, NA.
Notes:

☐ Auger, 2003, Ertl/RC, Die, 1/16, TBE15551, NA
Notes:

☐ Truck, 2003, Ertl/RC, Die, 1927 Graham Delivery Truck, "John Deere," 1/25, Bank No. 116, TBE15499, NA
Notes:

☐ Combine, 2004, Ertl/RC, Die, 97605TS, 2 heads, 1/32, TBE-15358, NA
Notes:

☐ Combine, 1991, Ertl, Die, 12A, 50th Anniversary Collector Ed, 5601DA, NIB $35
☐ ALSO SAME, Except Shelf Model, $20-30
Notes:

☐ Combine, 1995, Weber, Custom, 9600, Corn, Grain, RC Heads, Auctions Only, NA
Notes:

☐ Combine, 2001, Ertl/RC, Die, Model 45, Prestige Vintage Series, TBE15195, NIB $85
Notes:

☐ Corn Picker, 1952, Carter, PS, Model 227, Mounted, Fits 60-730, 2 Decal Variations, Excellent-NIB $220-375
☐ Corn Picker, 1961, Carter, PS, Model 227, Mounted, Fits 3010, Long Nose, TY 1007, Excellent-NIB $300-495
Notes:

☐ Corn Picker, 1990, Weber, Custom, 1 Row Model 18, Left Hand Or Right Hand, On Ertl Anniversary A, Custom, Very Limited Production, NA
Notes:

☐ Corn Picker, 1990, Weber, Custom, 2 Row Model 237, Mounted on JD 70 Or 630, Custom, Very Limited Production, NA
Notes:

☐ Corn Picker, 1999, Ertl, Die, 237, Precision Series #14, With 4020, 5083KO, $165
Notes:

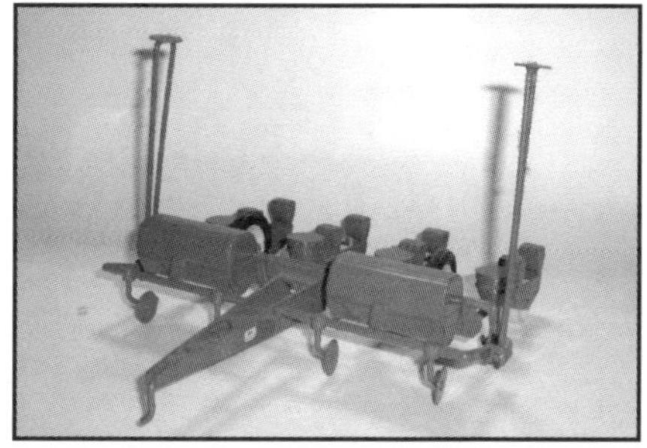

☐ Corn Planter, 1965, Ertl, Die, Four-Row Corn Planter Model 494, Various Hitches, Various No. Of Legs On Deer Decal, Other Varieties, 539, Exc-NIB $100-185
Notes:

☐ Corn Sheller, 1986, Riecke, Custom, Hand Crank, $60
Notes:

☐ **Cultivator, 1996, Ertl, Die, 856 Minimum Till, 6 Row, 5920DO, NIB $15**
Notes:

☐ **Dirt Scraper, 1968, Ertl, Die, K9, "C" Hitch, 549, New-NIB $165-290**
☐ **Dirt Scraper, 1965, Ertl, Die, K9, Green/Wht Bubble Box, Crank Hitch, 549, New-NIB $175-350**
☐ **Dirt Scraper, 1965, Ertl, Die, K9, Grn/Yellow Bubble Box, Crank Hitch, 549, New-NIB $175-350**
Notes:

☐ **Disc, 1950, Carter, PS, KBA, Green, No Wheels, Drag Type, Excellent-NIB $100-220**
Notes:

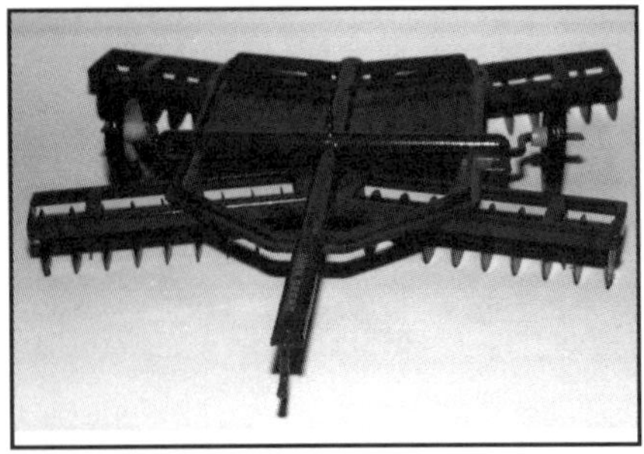

☐ **Disc, 1958, Ertl, Die, RWA, Metal Rims, Diecast Wheels, White And Black Box, Excellent-NIB $140-290**
☐ **Disc, 1960, Carter, Die, RWA, 3 Holes In Wheels Tin Strap Holds Up, Excellent-NIB $165-295**
Notes:

☐ **Disc, 1964, Ertl, Die, RWA, Plastic Wheels Or Rims, Various Axle Ends, C Hitch, 528, Excellent-NIB $40-90**
☐ **ALSO SAME, Except Plastic Rims, Bubble Box, Crank Hitch, 528, Excellent-NIB $60-125**
Notes:

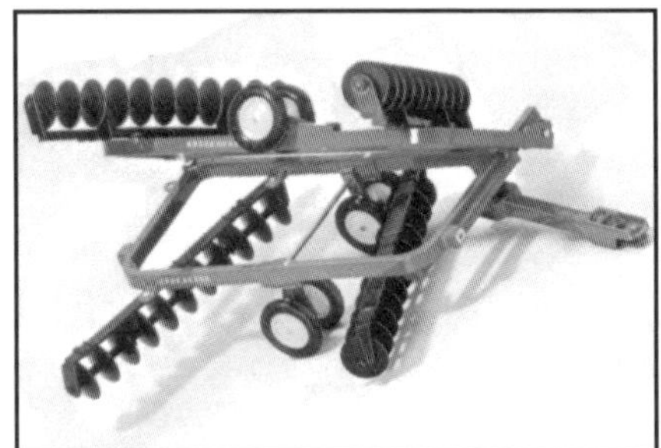

☐ **Disc, 1973, Ertl, Die, Model 220, Green And Yellow, Center Fold Tandem, 583, Excell-NIB $65-110**
☐ **ALSO SAME, Except 1978, Ertl, Green And Black, H-Frame Filled In Solid At Front, 583, Excellent-NIB $40-70**
Notes:

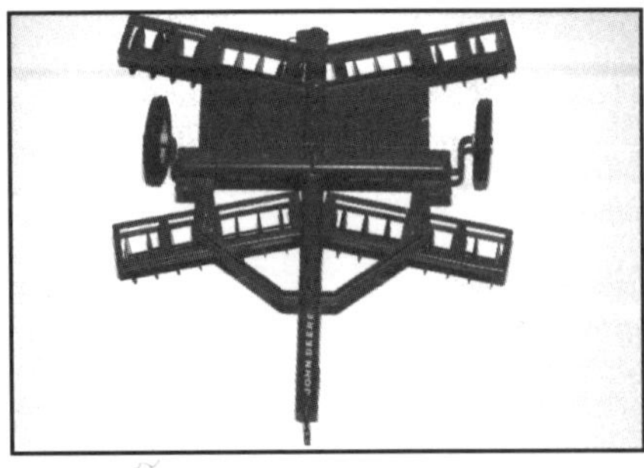

☐ **Disc, 1978, Sigomec, Die, Crank-Type Hitch Or 3 Point Hitch, 2530, Excellent-NIB $45-65**
☐ **ALSO RWA Wheel Disc, 2700, Excellent-NIB $40-65**
Notes:

☐ **Disc, 1990, Ertl, Die, Non-Folding, 4 Wheels, 5602DO, NIB $20**
Notes:

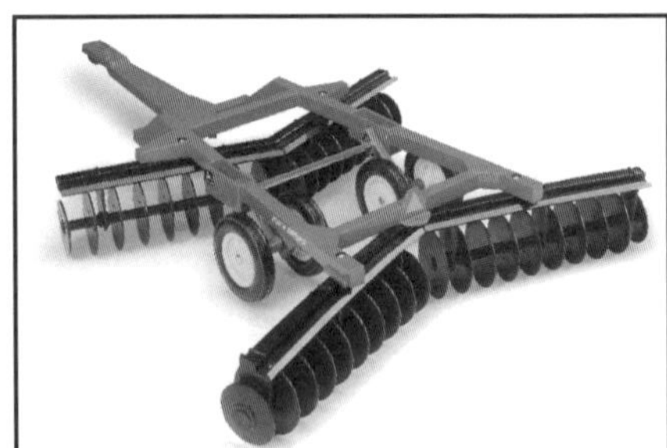

☐ **Disc, 1999, Ertl, Die, 15054, $18**
Notes:

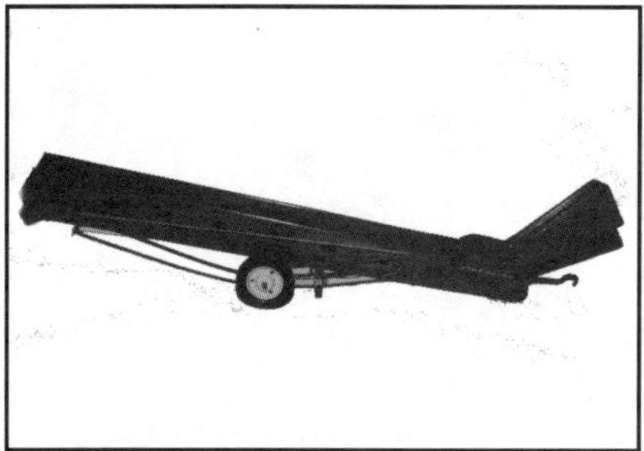

☐ **Elevator, 1960, Carter, PS, Model 300, Oval Holes In Sides, Excellent-NIB $185-300**
Notes:

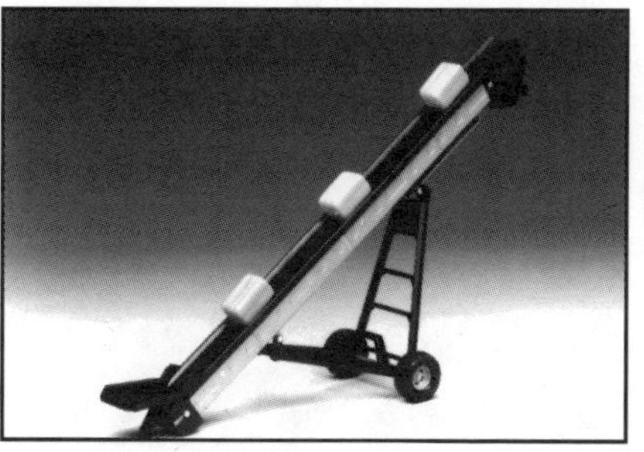

☐ **Elevator, 1991, Ertl, Die, With Bales, 5609DO, Excellent-NIB $20-35**
Notes:

☐ **Though the detail on this Ertl gas engine does not rival detail in general on the Precision Series toys the company is making, there is a great more than there used to be, which is what collectors today are asking for. For example, just check the next (and most valuable) engine, the Vindex, which has little detail.**

☐ **Engine, 1930, Vindex, CI, Gas, Stationary, On Cart, Green, Excellent $700**
☐ **ALSO, REPRO Except 1969, OTT, CA, Excellent-NIB $35-45**
☐ **ALSO, REPRO Except 1978, PTW, CA, Excellent-NIB $35-45**
☐ **ALSO, REPRO Except 1987, PC, CA, Excellent-NIB $35-45**
Notes:

☐ **Engine, 1981, Gray, Korloy, Portable Gas Engine Model E, Also On Steel Wheels, Not Always Thought Of As John Deere, NIB $35**
Notes:

☐ **Engine, 1991, Ertl, Die, "1991 National Farm Toy Show," Yellow Stripe On Flywheel, Collector Insert, 4986DO, Excellent-NIB $10-15**
Notes:

☐ **Engine, 1992, SpecCast, Die, "1992 Nashville Show," 5645DA, $20**
Notes:

☐ **Engine, 1992, SpecCast, Die, JDM064, NIB $15**
Notes:

☐ **Engine, AMT, Power Unit Based on John Deere D Engine, $32**
Notes:

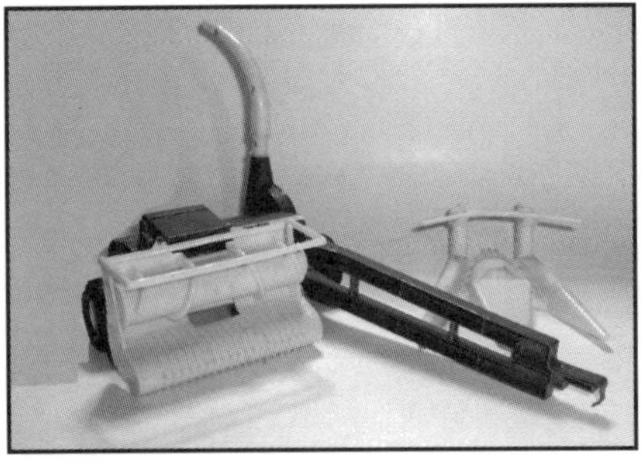

☐ Forage Harvester, 1984, Ertl, Die, Interchangeable Heads, 509EO, $25
Notes:

☐ Forage Harvester, 1996, Ertl, Die, 3950, Green Head, 509DP, $20
Notes:

☐ Grain Box Only, 1930, Vindex, CI, With Separate Seat, Excellent $300
Notes:

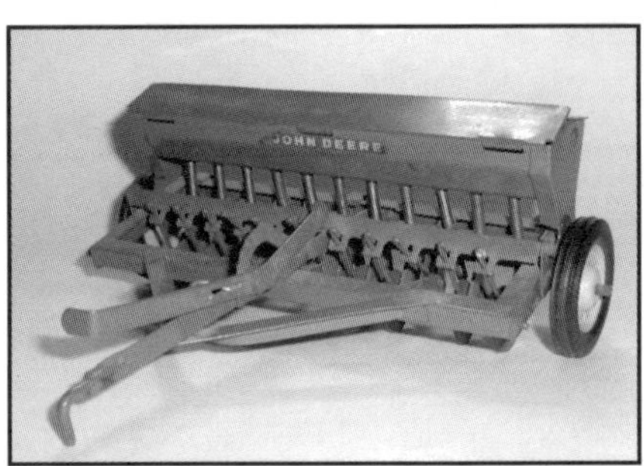

☐ Grain Box Bench Seat Only, 1930, Vindex, CI, Bench Seat For Vindex Grain Box, Excellent $300
Notes:

☐ Grain Drill, 1930, Vindex, CI, Van Brunt, Red, With Plate Discs, Rare, $2400
Notes:

☐ Grain Drill, 1952, Carter, PS, Green Lids, Various Decals, Excellent-NIB $180-325
Notes:

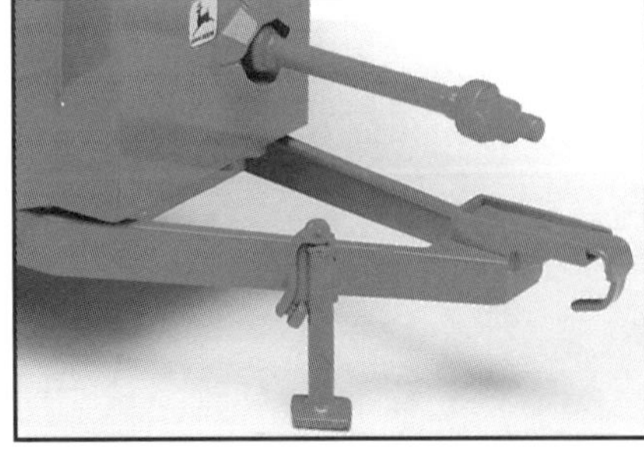

☐ Grain Drill, 1960, Carter, PS, Yellow Lids, Green Disc Openers, Excellent-NIB $200-420
☐ ALSO SAME, Except Yellow Lids, Silver Disc Openers, Excellent-NIB $245-450
Notes:

☐ One reason toy farmers love modern toys is because of how much detail they give, like with this grinder-mixer.
Notes:

☐ Grinder-Mixer, 1999, Ertl, Die, 5002, NIB $23
Notes:

□ Harrow, 1986, Nygren, SC/SS, Spring Tooth Pull-Type, (As Above), Or Spike Tooth, 3-Point Hitch, Two, Three- Or Four Section, Custom, NA
Notes:

□ Hay Loader, 1930, Vindex, CI, Red, $3600
Notes:

□ Hay Loader, 1990, Rouch, Custom, Highly Detailed, Working Cylinder, NA
Notes:

□ Hay Mower, 1961, Ertl, Die, Model 37, Crank Hitch, Bubble Box, 546, Excellent-NIB $80-150
ALSO SAME, Except 1966, C Hitch, Closed Box, 546, Excellent-NIB $70-110
Notes:

□ Hay Mower, Nolt, Custom, $110
Notes:

□ Hay Rack, 1930, Vindex, CI, Green, Separate From Running Gear And Team, Excellent $750
Notes:

□ One of the reasons the Vindex John Deere hay loader is so valuable is because of its age, because few of them were made, but also because of the detail, as shown above, which was unusual for the time.
Notes:

□ Hay Rake, 1991, Haag, Custom, Side Delivery Hay Rake, Low Wheels Style, Custom, NA
Notes:

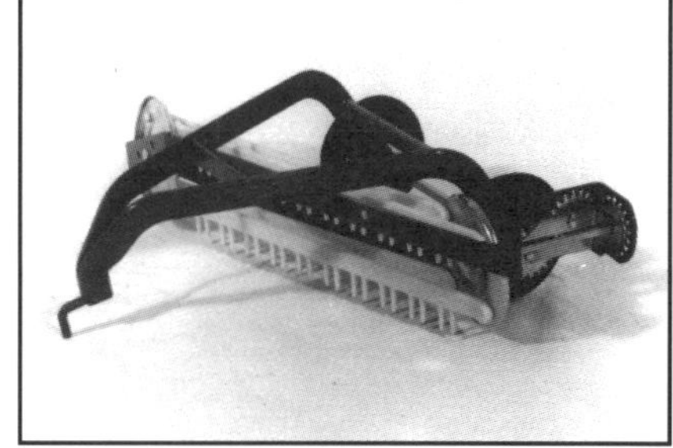

□ Hay Rake, 1991, Ertl, Die, 5686DO, NIB $15
Notes:

☐ Note the amazing detail and the lifelike forms of the horses in this Foxfire horse-drawn dump rake.
Notes:

☐ Hay Rake, 1998, Ertl, Die Cast And Cold-Cast Porcelain, Horse Drawn Dump, "Envying No Man," Red Rake With Yellow Wheels, Foxfire, Driver, 5066CO, NIB $80
Notes:

☐ Horses, 1930, Vindex, CI, Black Team, Fits On Wagons Or Spreader, $1000
Notes:

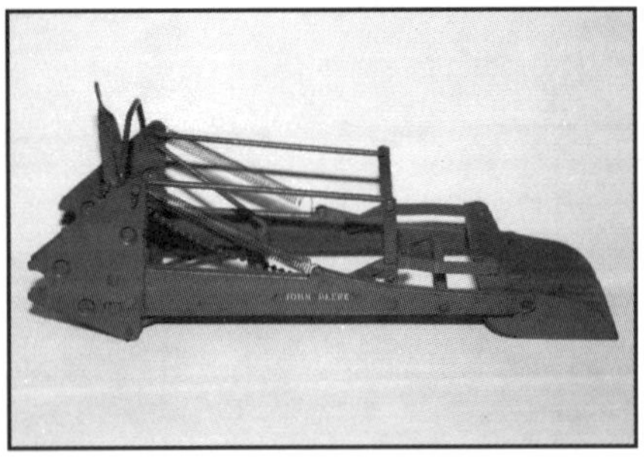

☐ Loader, 1957, Carter, PS, Model 45, Same, But No Axle Clips, Fits 620, Excellent-NIB $150-235
☐ ALSO SAME, Except 1952, Fits Early 60 Using Axle Clips, Excellent-NIB $150-265
Notes:

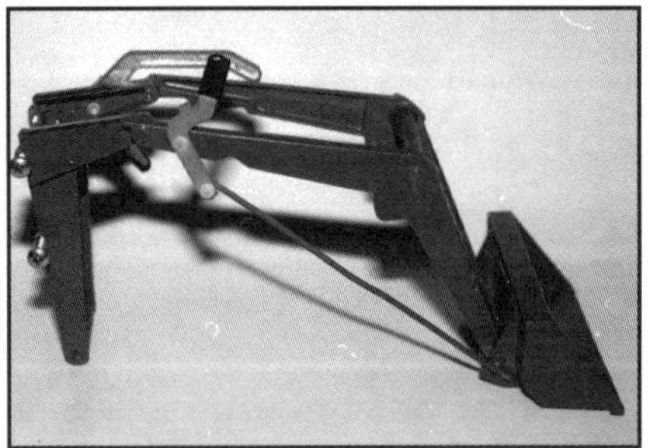

☐ Loader, 1962, Ertl, Die, Model 48, Fits 3010 And 3020 Series, Excellent-NIB $80-120
Notes:

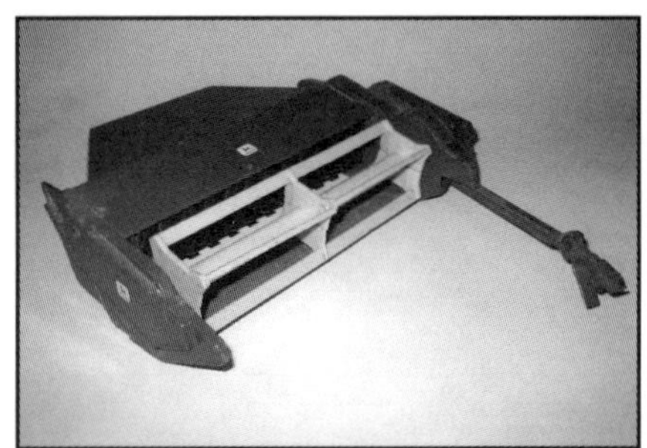

☐ Mower-Conditioner, 1975, Ertl, Die, Green With Yellow Reel, 596DO, Excellent-NIB $20-30
Notes:

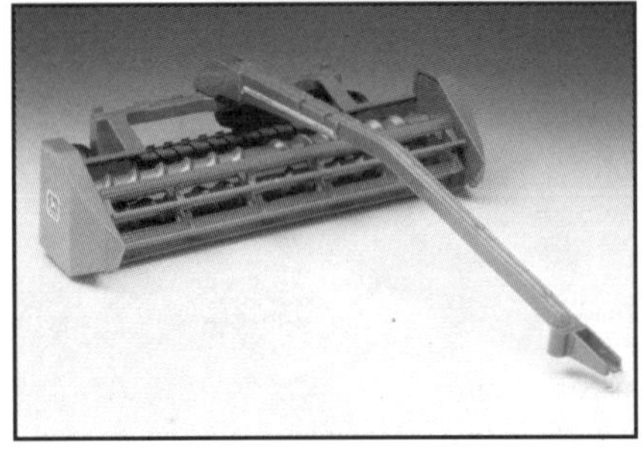

☐ Mower-Conditioner, 1991, Ertl, Die, Model 1600, Pivoting Hitch And Rotating Beater Bars, 5630, NIB $22
☐ ALSO 1996, Model, 1600A, NIB $20
Notes:

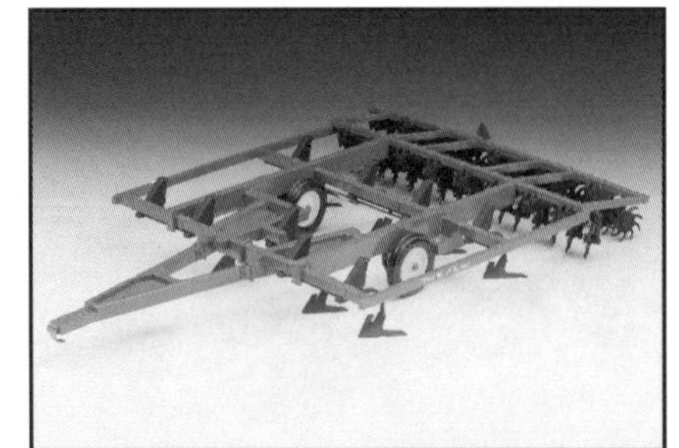

☐ Mulch Tiller, 1994, Ertl, Die, Model 550, 5711, NIB $20
Notes:

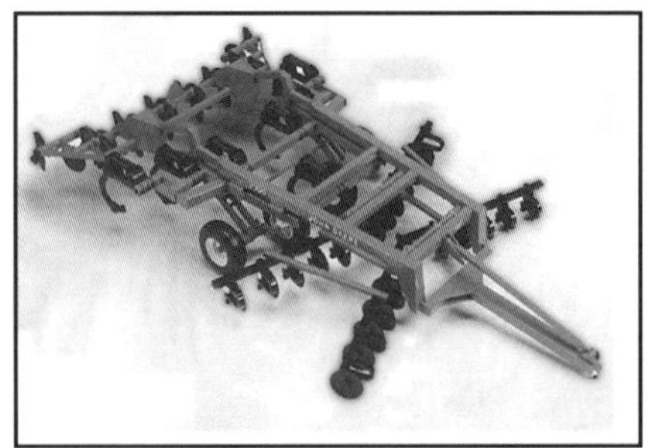

☐ Mulch Ripper, 2002, Ertl/RC, Die, TBE15356, NIB $22
Notes:

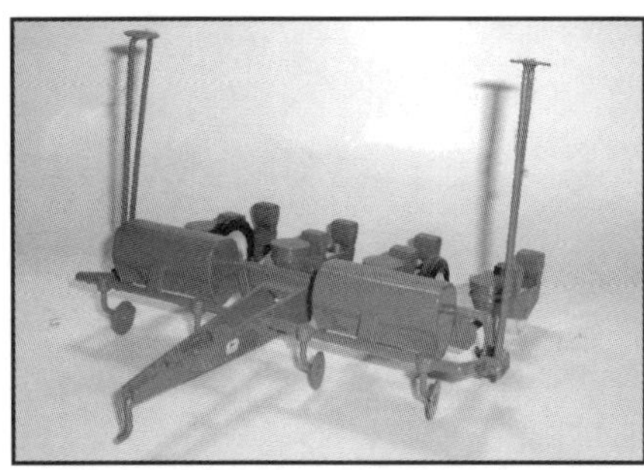

☐ Planter, 1965, Ertl, Die, 495, 4-Row, Crank Hch, 539, Ex-NIB $100-235
☐ ALSO SAME, Except 1970, C Hitch, 539, Excell-NIB $100-185
Notes:

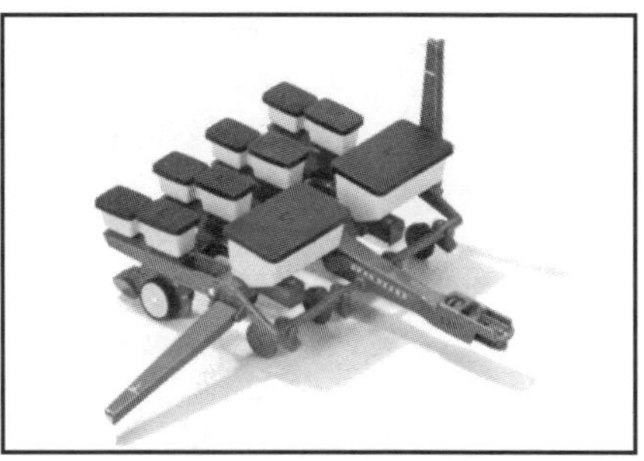

☐ Planter, 1978, Ertl, Die, Model 7000, 4 Row, Various Decals & Rivets, 595EO, NIB $50
Notes:

☐ Planter, 1996, Ertl, Die, 494A, #9 Vintage Precision Classic, 5838CO, NIB $100
Notes:

☐ Planter, 1998, Ertl, Die, 1700, Toolbar, 5177DO, NIB $20
☐ ALSO 1999, 5177 DA, NIB $22
Notes:

☐ Plow, 1930, Vindex, CI, 3 Bottom Pull Type, Green, Excellent $1700
☐ ALSO SAME, Except 1998, ScaMo, Reproduction, NIB $180
Notes:

☐ Plow, 1950, Carter, PS, 2 Bottom, Crank And Cylinder, Tail Wheel Varieties, Excellent-NIB $160-285
Notes:

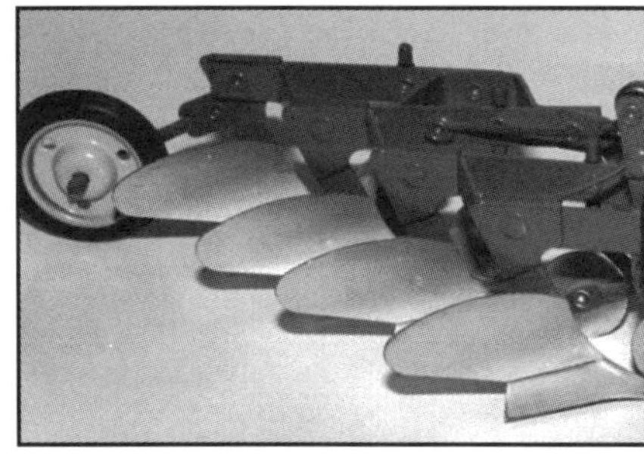

☐ Plow, 1956, Carter, PS, 4 Bottom, Model 3PH, Mounted, 2 Coulter Variations, Excellent-NIB $140-210
Notes:

☐ Plow, 1960, Ertl, Die, F66OH, 4 Bottom, Pull Type, Wheel And Tire Varieties, Angle Brace Varieties, Diecast Wheels, 527, Excellent-NIB $150-300
☐ ALSO SAME, Except Plastic Wheels, Excellent-NIB $60-125
Notes:

☐ Plow, 1970, Ertl, Die, F66OH, 4 Bottom, Plastic Rims, Tire Varieties, Brace Or No Brace, Bubble Bx, 527, Exc-NIB $60-125
Notes:

☐ Plow, 1976, Ertl, Die, 6 Bottom, Swivel Wheels Or Not, 525, NIB $20
Notes:

☐ Plow, 1978, Sigomec, Die, 5 Bottom, 3 Point, No Tail Wheel, 2800, Excellent-NIB $40-65
☐ ALSO Rerelease In 1992, 2806, Excellent-NIB $50-70
Notes:

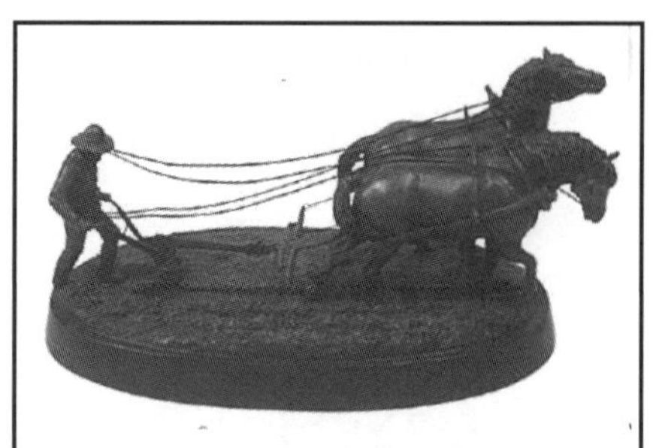

☐ Plow, 1987, Lalonda, Brass, Walking Plow With Team Of Horses & Driver, John Deere 150th Anniversary, NIB $700
Notes:

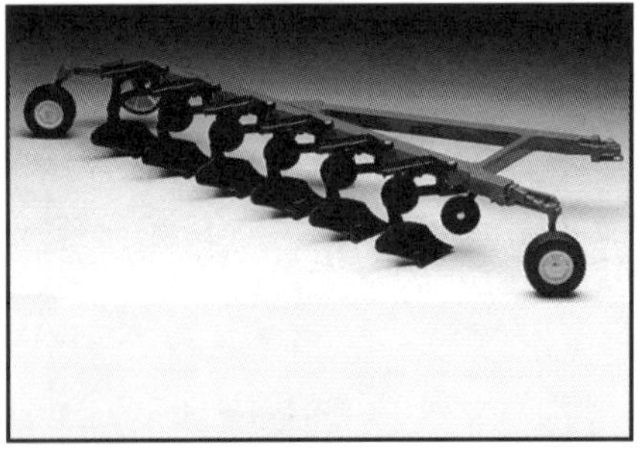

☐ Plow, 1982, Ertl, Die, 6 Bottom, Semi-Mounted, 3 Wheels, 525DO, NIB $20
Notes:

☐ Plow, 1991, Nolt, Custom, 2 Bottom, 3 Pt, Model 412, Excellent-NIB $75-100
Notes:

☐ Plow, 1991, Riecke, Custom, 3 Bottom, Pull Type, NIB $160
Notes:

☐ Plow, 1992, Stephan, Spin, Custom, 77H, 5-Bottom, PSJD04, $165
Notes:

☐ Plow, 1994, Ertl, Die, F145, Semi-Integrated Plow, 5 Bottom, Precision Classics, 5763CO, $125
Notes:

☐ Plow, 1994, Murphy, Die, Gilpen Sulky Plow, "1994 John Deere Parts Expo," NIB $40
Notes:

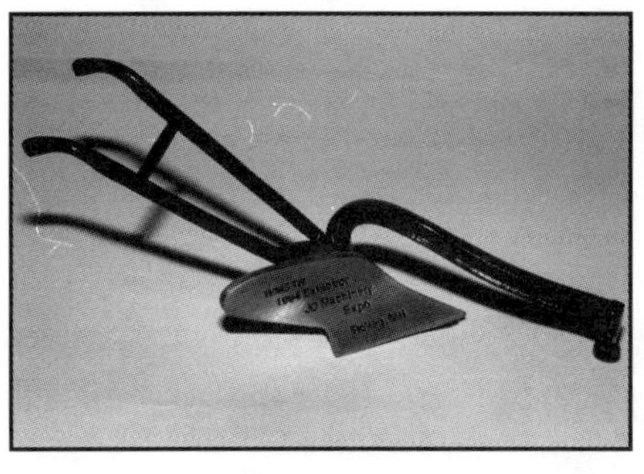

☐ **Plow, 1994, Plow, Walking, Western Minnesota Threshers' Reunion, Exhibitor, NIB $25**
Notes:

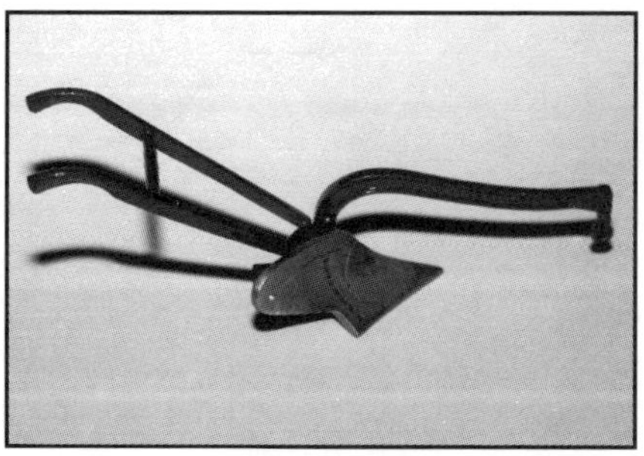

☐ **Plow, 1994, SpecCast, 100th Anniversary Minneapolis Branch, CUST299, Excellent-NIB $20-30**
Notes:

☐ **Plow, 1998, Ertl, Die, 3600, 6 Bottom, Semi-Mounted, With 3 Wheels, 5095DO, NIB $20**
Notes:

☐ **Plow, 2002, Nolt, 416 3-Point Hitch Plow, Custom, Excellent-NIB $75-100**
Notes:

☐ **Pressure Washer, 1991, SpecCast, Die, Special Promotion, 200 Made, 225G, $15**
Notes:

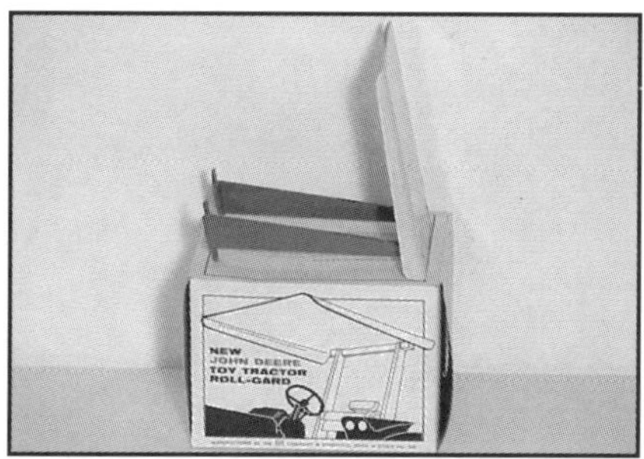

☐ **ROPS, 1962, Ertl, Die, Attachment For 3010/3020, Two Canopy Varieties, 548, Excellent-NIB $40-75**
Notes:

☐ **Rotary Mower, 1992, SpecCast, D, JDM046, Exc-NIB $20-32**
Notes:

☐ **Rotary Mower, 2002, Ertl, Die, MX7, 3 Point Hitch, Moving Parts, 15074, NIB $12**
Notes:

☐ **Rotary Hoe/Toolbar, 1996, Ertl, Die, Model 400, 5918DO, NIB $15**
Notes:

☐ Running Gear, Vindex, CI, For Hay Rack Or Grain Box, Excellent $300
Notes:

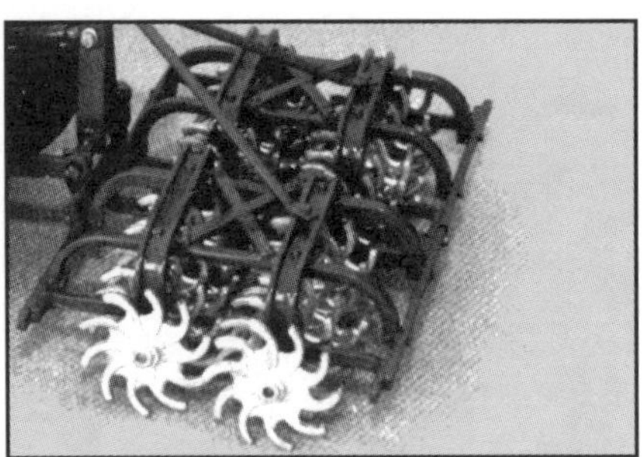

☐ Rotary Hoe, 2002, Nolt, 212-A 3-Point Hitch Plow, Custom, NIB $125
Notes:

☐ Skid Steer Loader, 1977, Ertl, Die, Green, And Black, 569, NA
☐ ALSO SAME, Except Green, 569, $20-25
☐ ALSO SAME, Except Yellow Rims, Or White Rims, 569 (See color section)
Notes:

☐ Skid Steer Loader, 2002, Ertl/RC, Plastic, Boom Arm Raises, Bucket Dumps, 15423, NIB $18
Notes:

☐ Skid Steer Loader, 2002, Ertl/RC, Die, Bucket Raises, Lowers, Dumps, 15144, NIB $15
Notes:

☐ Sprayer, 1994, SpecCast, Die, 6500, Self-Propelled, KZJD1, NIB $200
☐ ALSO SAME, Except WF, KCZO, NIB $200
Notes:

☐ Spreader, 1950, Carter, PS, Model K, Manure, Rubber Wheels, Short Levers, Excellent-NIB $100-220
Notes:

☐ Spreader, 1954, Carter, PS, Model K, Manure, Metal Rims And Rubber Tires, Excellent-NIB $100-225
Notes:

☐ Spreader, 1955, Carter, PS, Model L, Manure, Tin Wheels, Long Levers, Various Decals & Wheels, Excellent-NIB $100-220
Notes:

☐ Spreader, 1962, Ertl, Die, 44, Manure, No Gear Drive, Closed Box, Plastic Wheels, 534, Excellent-NIB $30-50
☐ ALSO SAME, But Metal Wheels, Closed Box, Exc-NIB $40-80
☐ ALSO SAME, But "44" Decals, Bubble Box, Exc-NIB $65- 140
Notes:

☐ Spreader, 1970, Ertl, Die, 44, No "44" Decals, Large JD Decals, C-Type Hitch, 534, Excellent-NIB $30-40
Notes:

☐ Spreader, 1985, Ertl, Die, Hydra Push, Manure, 549EO, Excellent-NIB $14-20
☐ ALSO SAME, Except 2000, 549DO, NA
Notes:

☐ Spreader, 1991, Rouch, Model E, Highly Detailed, Four Or Two Wheels, Steel Or Rubber Wheels, Various Colors, Tractor Or Horse Hitch, Custom, NIB $300
Notes:

☐ Thresher, 1930, Vindex, CI, Silver, With Green Trim, $2500
Notes:

☐ Wagon, 1940, Made By Strombecker For Arcade, Wood, Flare Box, On Cast Iron Gear, Excellent-NIB $300-700
☐ ALSO, 1980, Swanson, Box Only, Repro Of Strombecker, NA
Notes:

☐ Wagon, 1965, Ertl, Die, 112, Chuck, Plastic Wheels, Bubble Box, 3 Varieties, 533, Excellent-NIB $60-135
Notes:

☐ Wagon, 1970 Ertl, PS, Flare, Non-Removable Box, Edges Not Rolled, PI Rims, 5 Vars, 529EO, Excellent-NIB $20-35
☐ ALSO SAME, Except 1965, Cast Rims, Boy Box, Excellent-NIB $85-220
Notes:

☐ Wagon, 1970, Ertl, Die, Forage, Non-Removable Box, Closed Box, No Numbers, 5 Vars, 533, Excellent-NIB $30-60
Notes:

□ Wagon, 1981, Ertl, PS, Barge, Non-Removable Box, 529, Excellent-NIB $15-30
Notes:

□ Wagon, 1984, Ertl, PS, Bale Throw, 522EO, Excellent-NIB $10-16
□ ALSO SAME, Except Remake, 1989, 522DO, NIB $15
Notes:

□ Wagon, 1986, Ertl, D & SS, Forage, Flat Tongue, Plastic Sides And Top, 510, NIB $15
Notes:

□ Wagon, 1988, NB&K, SC, High Sides, "John Deere Moline, Ill" Decals, Red Seat, Running Gear, Horse Or Tractor Tongue, NA
Notes:

□ Wagon, 1990, Murphy, Die, Horse-Drawn, "John Deere 1990" Cast Under Seat, $25
□ Wagon, 1990, Murphy, Die, Farm, DSCAT1562, $20
□ Wagon, 1994, Murphy, Die, JD Expo '94, "New Orleans After-market 2000," DS0544, NIB $30
Notes:

□ Wagon, 1991, Ertl, Die And Plastic, Hay, Brown Hay Rack With Wood Grain Design, Black Running Gear, 12 Green Bales, No JD On It, 5674, Exc-NIB $8-20
Notes:

□ Wagon, 2000, Ertl, Die, TBE15133, Barge, Precision Classic, $45
Notes:

□ Wagon, 2000, Ertl, Die, Gravity, TBE15125, NIB $20
Notes:

□ Wagon, 2001, Ertl/RC, Die, Barge, 15203, NIB $15
Notes:

□ Wagon, 2001, Ertl/RC, Die, Precision Classic, No 19, 15134, NIB $42
Notes:

□ Combine, 1970, Ertl, Die, 6600, Chain Drive Auger And Reel, Silver Bar Or No Bar Through Reel, 558, Excellent-NIB $220-350
□ ALSO SAME Except Chain Drive Auger, Gear Drive Reel, 558, Excellent-NIB $180-320

Begin 1/24 Scale

□ Combine, 1978, Ertl, Die, 6600, Gear Drive Auger & Reel, Plastic Reel, 558, Excellent-NIB $115-185
□ ALSO SAME But Rears Have Lugs, 558, Excell-NIB $175-275
□ ALSO SAME Except No Ertl Mark On Casting, NIB $275
Notes:

□ Combine, 1978, Ertl, Die, Titan Or Titan II, Yellow Top, Varied Lettering, Drive Chains, 524, NIB $100
Notes:

□ Combine, 1984, Ertl, Die, Titan, Re-issued in 1984 With Corn Head, 536CO, Excell-NIB $60-85
Notes:

□ Combine, 1987, Ertl, Die, Titan II, Corn & Bean Heads, Green Top, 582CO, Excellent-NIB $50-70
Notes: :

□ Plow, 1973, Ertl, Plastic, 6 Bottom, Steerable, Nice Detail, Kit, 8012, Excellent-NIB $10-25
Notes:

□ Wagon, 1973, Ertl, Plastic, Barge, Kit, 8006, Excellent-NIB $10-15
Notes:

□ Combine, 1989, Ertl, Die, 9600, Self-Propelled, John Deere 9600 1989 Special Edition, 546CA, NIB $45
Notes:

Begin 1/28 Scale

☐ **Combine, 1990, Ertl, Die, 9500, With 2 Heads, Black Reel, 546CO, NIB $35**
Notes:

☐ **Combine, 1998, Ertl, Die, 9510 Maximizer, 5171CO, NIB $35**
Notes:

☐ **Thresher, 1994, SpecCast, Die, JDMO39, NIB $55**
☐ **ALSO SAME, Except Limited Edition, JDM040, NIB $65**
Notes:

☐ **Thresher, 1996, SpecCast, Die, On Rubber, JDM079, NIB $55**
Notes:

☐ **Baler, 1998, Ertl, Die, Square, Model #100, 5082DO, NIB $10**
Notes:

☐ **Baler, 2000, Ertl, Die, Model 590, 15031H, NIB $10**
Notes:

☐ **Combine, 2000, Ertl, Die, Model 2266, European, TBE12017, NIB $32**
Notes:

☐ **Combine, 2000, Ertl, Die, 9750STS, Precision Series II, 15036, NIB $100**
Notes:

☐ **Forage Harvestor, 1998, Ertl, Die, Model 6850, 5129DO, NIB $15**
Notes:

□ **Forage Harvestor, 1999, Ertl, Die, Model 6650, With Corn Head, 5129, NIB $18**
Notes: :

□ **Spreader, 1989, Ertl, Die, Manure, Hydra Push, 5577, NIB $8**
Notes:

□ **Wagon, 1989, Ertl, Plastic, PTO, Dump, 5623, $5-10** *Notes:*

□ **Combine,SpecCast, Pewter, 9750STS, 8 Row Head, 1/43 Scale, NIB $35**
Notes:

(Photo Courtesy Of SpecCast)

□ **Engine, 1992, SpecCast, Pewter, "Power Tech," JDM124, NIB $45**
Notes:

(Photo Courtesy Of SpecCast)

□ **Engine, 1993, SpecCast, Pewter, 1/43 Scale, Nash Pts E, JDM071, NIB $15**
Notes:

□ **Engine, 1994, SpecCast, Die, Waterloo Boy Type H, With Skid 3 1/2," JDM043, NIB $20**
Notes:

□ **Spreader, 1992, Ertl, Die, Manure, Vintage, Working Beaters, 5654EO, Excellent-NIB $3-5**
Notes:

□ **Thresher, 1994, SpecCast, Custom, Regular, JDM039, NIB $50**
□ **ALSO SAME, Except Special Edition, (Shown), JDM040, NIB $55**
Notes:

□ Wagon, 1999, Ertl, Die, Flare Box Wagon, 33530, Exc-NIB $3-6
Notes:

□ Combine, '81, Ertl, Die, SP, 985 Hydro 4, Square Cab, 985 Front Of Decal, 1634, Exc-NIB $18-28
□ ALSO, SAME But "985" Rear Of Decals, Excellent-NIB $18-28
□ ALSO SAME, Except 1980, In Plastic Bubble, Exc-NIB $18-28

□ Combine, 1984, Ertl, Die, Model 885 European Combine, Hydro 4, 1994EO, Excellent-NIB $12-20
Notes:

□ Combine, 1987, Ertl, Die, 4425, 506EO, NIB $25
Notes:

□ Combine, 1999, SpecCast, Pewter, 9610, JDM118, NIB $35
Notes:

(Photo Courtesy Of SpecCast)

□ Combine, SpecCast, Pewter, 9750 Rotary, JDM139, NIB $35
□ ALSO SAME, Except Part Of Pen Set, NIB $40
Notes:

(Photo Courtesy Of SpecCast)

□ Excavator, 2002, SpecCast, Pewter, 200LC, JDM152, NIB $35
□ ALSO SAME, Except Part Of Pen Set, NIB $35
Notes

(Photo Courtesy Of SpecCast)

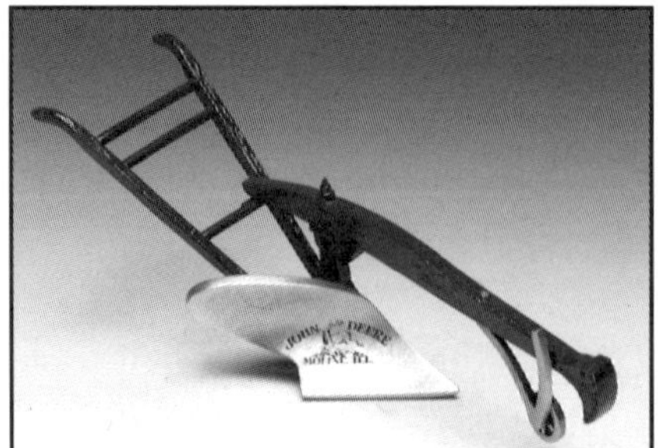

□ Plow, SpecCast, "John Deere Moline III," JDM112, NIB $15
Notes:

(Photo Courtesy Of SpecCast)

□ Skid Steer, SpecCast, Pewter, 250, JDM129, NIB $22
□ ALSO SAME, Except On Pen Set, JDM133, NIB $25
Notes:

(Photo Courtesy Of SpecCast)

☐ Ammonia Tank, 1986, Ertl, Die, 4-Wheels, White Or Yllw Tank, W/ Or WO "Anhydrous Ammonia," Yellow Wheels, 5551FO, NIP $5
☐ Ammonia Tank, 1996, ED, 7392, NIP $5
☐ Ammonia Tank, 1994, Ertl, Die, 3 Variations, 4324, NIP $5

Begin 1/64 Scale

☐ Auger, 1986, Ertl, Plastic, Generic, 5559FO And 5555, NIP $12
Notes:

☐ Bale Processor, 1987, Ertl, Die, Two Wheels, Yellow Stripes, Generic, 5568, NIP $6
Notes:

☐ Baler, 1985, Ertl, Die, 535, Round, Green & Yellow, 577, NIP $10
☐ ALSO SAME, Except 1996, All Green, NIP $6
☐ ALSO SAME, Except 1993, Revised, Graphics, All Green, 577FP, NIP $4
Notes:

☐ Baler, 1996, Ertl, Die, 338, Square, Green Pickup, 5646, NIP $4
☐ ALSO SAME, Except Yellow Pickup, 5646FO, NIP $5
Notes:

☐ Baler, 2001, Ertl/RC, Die, Round, TBE15318, NIP $4
Notes:

☐ Cart, Ertl, Die, Model 1900 Commodity, 200 Made, 15082, NIP $7
Notes:

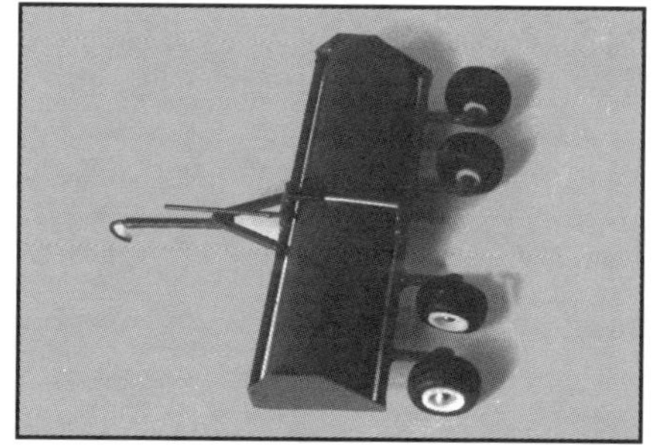

☐ Chopper, Van Hove, Stalk Chopper, Custom, NIP $25
Notes:

☐ Combine, 1988, Gunning, SC, Self-Propelled Model 55 Or Model 95, With Grain Head, Or Two- Or Three-Row Corn Heads, Custom, NIP $45
Notes:

□ **Combine, 1988, Gunning, SC, Self-Propelled Model 105 With Grain Head, Custom, NIP $45**
Notes:

□ **Combine, 1996, Ertl, Die, 95, 4 Row Corn Head, 5819, NIP $7**
□ **ALSO SAME, Except 1997, 5819FO, NIP $7**
□ **ALSO SAME, Except 2000, 5819EO, NIP $7**
Notes:

□ **Combine, C&G, Pull-Type, Custom, NIP $40**
Notes:

□ **Combine, 1990, 9500, Two Heads, 5604EO, NIP $25**
Notes:

□ **Combine, 1997, Ertl, Die, 9610, 12 Row Corn Hd, 5809, NIP $22**
Notes:

□ **Combine, C&D, Kit, 9610 Maximizer, NA**
Notes:

□ **Combine, 8 Row Corn Head, C.T.S. Model, NIP $16**
Notes:

□ **Combine, 1999, E, D, 9750 STS, 12 C/30' Bean Head, 15038, NIP $12**
Notes:

□ **Combine, 2002, Ertl/RC, Die, STS Combine D-Kit, TBE15430, NIP $12**
Notes:

□ Corn Picker, 1988, Nygren, SC, 2-Row Model 200, Custom, NIP $20

□ Corn Picker, 1986, Nygren, SC, 2-Row Model 227, Mounts On Ertl 1/64 JD 60, Custom, NIP $20

Notes:

□ Corn Picker, 1988, Standi, Plastic, 3-Row Pull-Type, NIP $6

Notes:

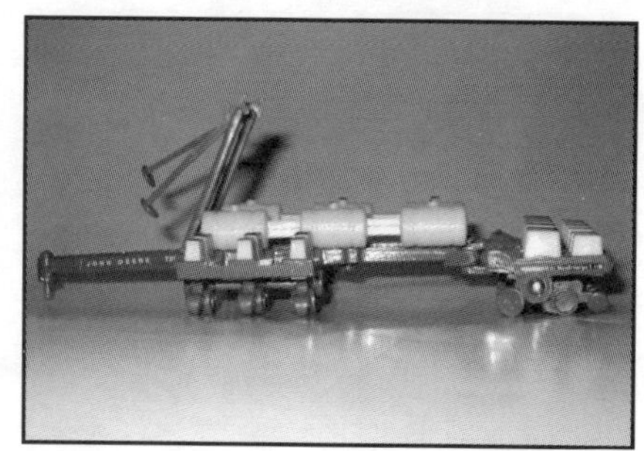

□ Corn Planter, 1986, Ertl, Die, Model 7200 12-Row Folding, Various Countries Of Manufacture, 576FO, Or 576-7HFO, NIP $10

Notes:

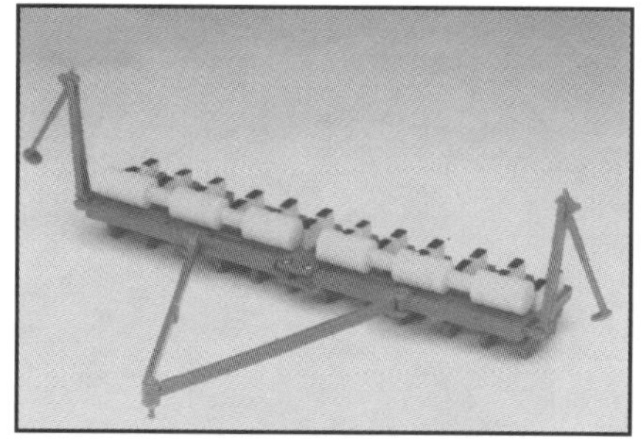

□ Corn Planter, 1986, Ertl, Die, 12 Row, Folding, 576, NIP $12

Notes:

□ Cotton Picker, 1997, Ertl, Die, Model 9976, 5765EO, NIP $10

□ ALSO SAME, Except Memphis Edition, NIP $15

Notes:

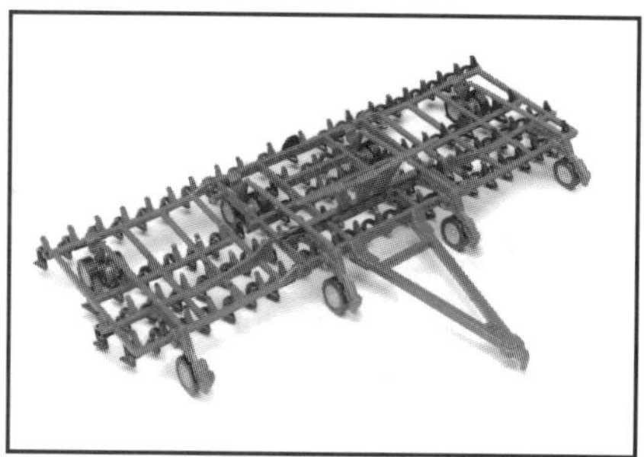

□ Cultivator, 2001, Ertl/RC, Die, Chisel Plow, TBE15081, NIP $8

Notes:

□ Disc, 1997, Ertl, Die, Winged, TBE5615, NIP $5

Notes:

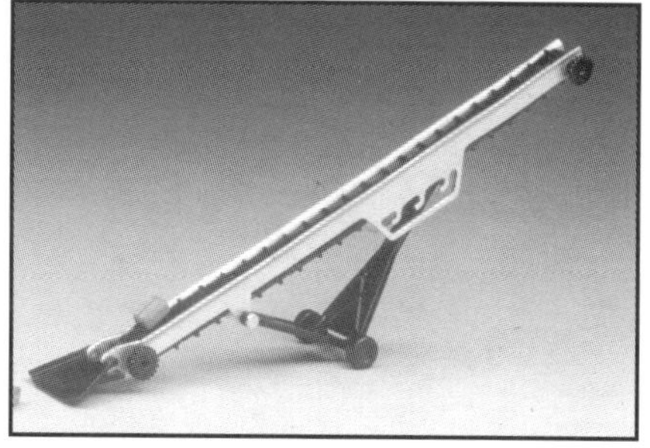

□ Elevator, 1992, Ertl, Die, Belted, 5661, NIP $10

□ Elevator, 1989, Ertl, Die, Belted, JD Card, Generic, 5609, NIP $10

Notes:

□ Flail Mower, 1987, Nygren, SC, Flail Stalk Shredder, Custom, NIP $25

Notes:

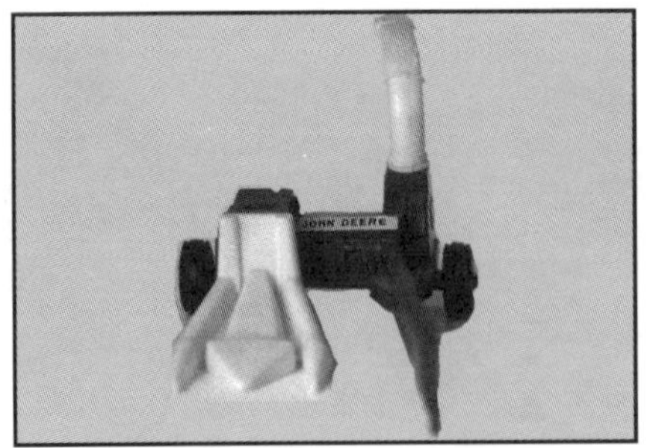

☐ Forage Blower, 1996, Ertl, Die, 150A, 5728, NIP $5
Notes:

☐ Forage Harvester, 1984, Ertl, Die, Yellow Corn Head, 566FO, NIP $8
☐ ALSO SAME, Except 1986, Green Head, 566, NIP $7
☐ ALSO SAME, Except Revised 1993, 566FO, NIP $7
Notes:

☐ Forage Harvester, 1993, Ertl, Die, 6910, Self-Pr, 5658EO, NIP $16
Notes:

☐ Forage Harvester, 1996, Ertl, Die, Model 3950, 566FR, NIP $5
Notes:

☐ Grain Cart, 1986, Ertl, Die, 5556FO, NIP $5
Notes:

☐ Grain Cart, Model 500, With Fold-Down Auger, 5565FP, NIP $5
Notes:

☐ Grain Drill, 1989, Ertl, Die, Model 8300, Yellow Top, Black Openers, 5528EO, NIP $5
Notes:

☐ Grain Drill, C&D, No-Till, Custom, NIP $35
Notes:

☐ Grain Drill, 1999, Ertl, Die, Model 1560, No Till, 15016, NIP $5
Notes:

□ Grinder Mixer, 2001, Ertl/RC, Die, TBE15319, NIP $5
Notes:

□ Hay Rake, 1984, Ertl, Die, Yellow Reel, Generic, 5751, NIP $5
□ Hay Rake, 1996, Ertl, Die, Green Reel, (Shown Above) 5751FR, NIP $5
Notes:

□ Hay Rake, Moore, Combination, NIP $7
Notes:

□ Mixer Mill, 1986, Ertl, Die, Grinder, Generic, 5554, NIP $6
Notes:

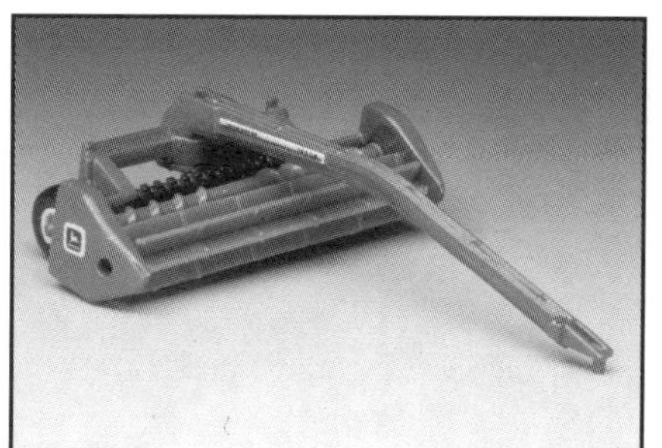

□ Mower Conditioner, 1996, Ertl, Die, 1600, 5657FP, NIP $4
□ ALSO SAME, Except 1992, 5657, NIP $5
□ ALSO SAME, Except Revised Graphics, 5657, NIP $4
Notes:

□ Mulch Master, Model 550, 21 ft, 5727, NIP $5
Notes:

□ Mulch Tiller, 1986, Ertl, Die, 578, NIP $5
Notes:

□ Mulch Master, Model 2200, NIP $7
Notes:

□ Mulch Master Minimum Tillage Plow, 1994, Ertl, Die, 577, NIP $5
Notes:

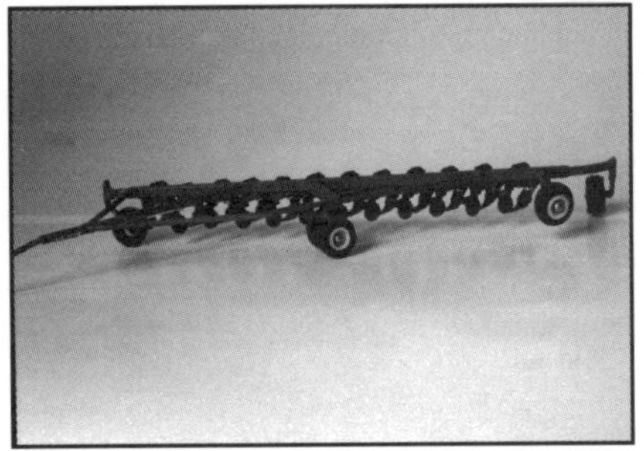

☐ **Plow, 12-Bottom, Generic, NIP $25**
Notes:

☐ **Plow, C&G, 12-Bottom, NIP $27**
Notes:

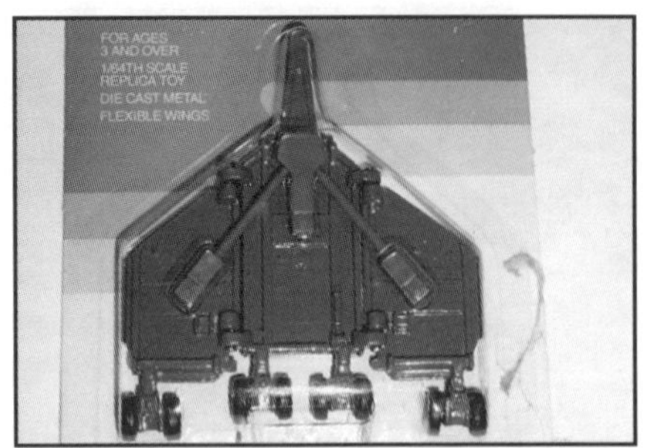

☐ **Rotary Cutter, 1993, Ertl, Die, Bat Wing, 5600FO, NIP $5**
Notes:

☐ **Sprayer, 1986, Ertl, Die, Two-Wheel Trailer Field Sprayer With Yellow Tank, 5553FO, NIP $5**
Notes:

☐ **Sprayer, 2001, Ertl/RC, Die, 4710, Self-Propelled, 15180, NIP $8**
Notes:

☐ **Sprayer, Model 4700, With Silver Side Tank, Error, 5752ER NIP $15**
ALSO SAME Except Yellow Tank (Correct Color), 5752FO, NIP $9
Notes:

☐ **Spreader, 1985, Ertl, Die, Hydra Push Manure, 574, NIP $4**
Notes:

☐ **Spreader, 1986, Ertl, Die, 876, Slurry, V-Tank, 5928, NIP $3**
Notes:

☐ **Spreader, 1986, Ertl, Plastic, Dry Fertilizer, Generic, 5558, NIP $6**
Notes:

□ Seeder, 2002, Ertl/RC, Die And Plastic, 1790 Split Row Planter, Folds Up For Road Transport, TBE15380, NIB $8
Notes:

□ Spreader, 1986, Ertl, Plastic, Liquid Manure, Generic, 5555, NIP $7
Notes:

□ Spreader, 1999, Ertl, Plastic, Liquid Manure, C&J Systems, 5185EO, NIP $5
Notes:

□ Spreader, 1999, Ertl, Die, Dry Fertilizer, 5184EO, NIP $5
Notes:

□ Trailer, 1986, Ertl, Plastic, Brown Bed, Generic, 5557, NIP $10
□ ALSO SAME Except Green Bed, NIP $16
Notes:

□ Trailer, 1992, Ertl, Die, Implement, (Does Not Include Skid-Steer), 5662FO, NIP $5
Notes:

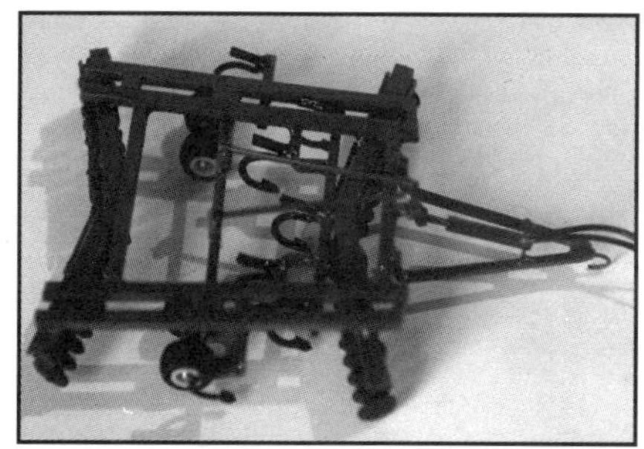

□ V-Ripper, Van Hove, Custom, 7-Point, NIP $39
Notes:

□ Wagon, 1984, Ertl, Die, Forage, Silver & Black Decals Or Black & Yellow Decals, 567, NIP $8
Notes:

□ Wagon, 1986, Ertl, Die, Gravity, Generic, 5552, NIP $8
Notes:

☐ **Wagon, 1986, Ertl, Plastic, K, Generic, 5560, NIP $6**
Notes:

☐ **Wagon, 1986, Ertl, Die, Model 500, Four-Wheel Hay Wagon With Rear Upright Rack, Wood Grain Deck, 5556, NIP $6**
Notes:

☐ **Wagon, 1987, Ertl, Die, Barge, Generic, Steerable, 5529, NIP $5**
Notes:

☐ **Wagon, 1995, Ertl, Die, Bale Throw, 5755FO, NIP $6**
Notes:

☐ **Wagon, 2001, Ertl/RC, Die, Gravity, TBE15317, NIP $4**
Notes:

☐ **Wagon, 2002, Ertl, Die, Flare-box, 5930, NIP $4**
Notes:

☐ **Combine, 1986, Ertl, Die, 2 Heads, Green Cab Top, Titan, 550, NIP $12**
Notes:

Begin 1/80 Scale

☐ **Combine, 1989, Micro-Machines, Die, Model Titan II, Self-Propelled, Hong Kong, NIP $2**
Notes:

Begin 1/87 Scale

☐ **Combine, 1997, Ertl, Die, Rice, CTS, Combine, 5029EO, NIP $10**
Notes:

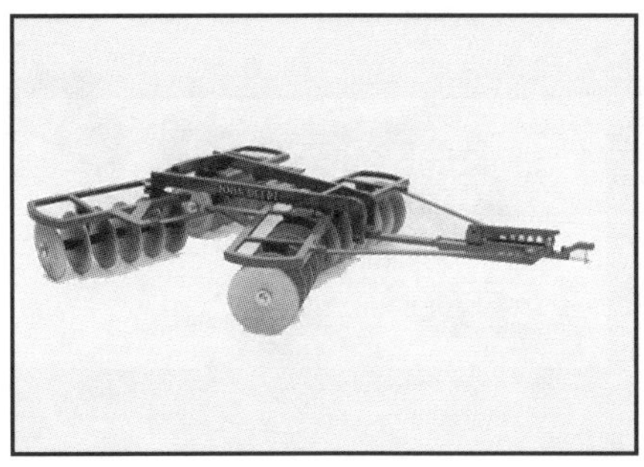

☐ **Disc, 1998, ScaMo, Die, KBA, FY-1007, NIB $70**
Notes:

Begin 1/8 Scale

☐ **Engine, 1994, Ertl, Die, Model E Battery Operated, With Sound, 5645, NIB $22**
Notes:

☐ **Gator, 2002, ScaMo, Die, Work-site Gator, FY-1023, NIB $100**
Notes:

☐ **Plow, 2000, ScaMo, Die, 4-Bottom Mounted, JLE1012A, NIB $70**
Notes:

☐ **Power Washer, 1991, Spec, Die, Model 225G, "1991 Parts Expo," Serial Number Plate On Bottom, CUST-101, NIB $18**
Notes:

☐ **Power Washer, 1992, Spec, Die, "1992 Nashville Show," Serial Number Plate On Bottom, CUST-152, NIB $30**
☐ **ALSO SAME, Except "Driven By A Vision Toronto 92," CUST-152, NIB $30**
Notes:

☐ **Spreader, 1998, ScaMo, Die, Manure, FY-1006, NIB $90**
Notes:

☐ **Wagon, 1996, SM, SCA, Steer-able, Die Cast Rims, Rubber Tires, FY-1001, NIB $70**
Notes:

☐ **Corn Planter, 2002, Lone Tree Creek, Brass, Deere & Mansur No. 999 Salesman Sample Series, Team of Horses, Ltd. To 250, 1/18 Scale, NA**
Notes:

☐ Backhoe/Loader, 1975, Ertl, Die, 310, 589DO, NIB $65
Notes:

Begin 1/16 Scale

☐ Backhoe Three-Point Hitch, 2001, 2001, Ertl/RC, Die, Attaches To Most 1/16 Tractors, 12196, NIB $12
Notes:

☐ Blade, 2000, Ertl, Die, Back Blade, 15052, NIB $10
Notes:

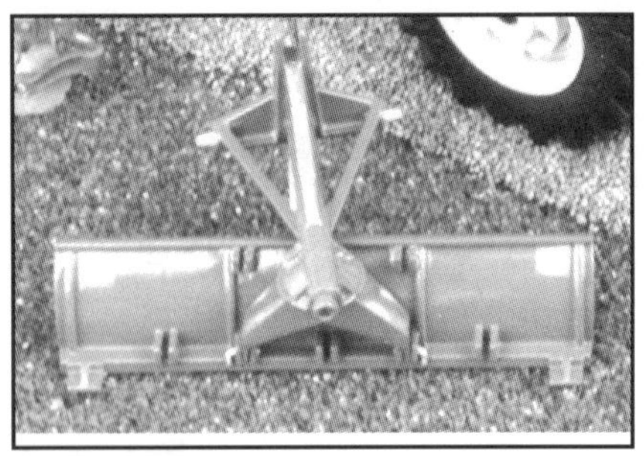

☐ Blade, Nolt, For 420 Industrial Tractor , NIB $40
Notes:

☐ Grader, 1987, Ertl, Die, 772B, With Cab, 511CO, Exc-NIB $35-45
Notes:

☐ Grader, 1995, Ertl, Die, 772BH, New Color & Decals, 511CP, Excellent-NIB $30-45
Notes:

☐ Grader, John Deere Decal But No Other Markings, NA
Notes:

☐ LI, 1994, SpecCast, Die, Tractor, Great American Farm Toy Sh, CUST266, Exc-NIB $30-35
☐ ALSO SAME, Except 1995, JDM 068, Excellent-NIB $30-35
☐ ALSO SAME, Except 1995, "Upper Canada Two-Cylinder Club," 200 Made, Exce-NIB $30-35
Notes:

☐ Lindeman, 2000, SpecCast, Die, Crawler On Steel Tracks, JDM 135, NIB $40
☐ ALSO SAME, Except 1998, JDM116, NIB $40
Notes:

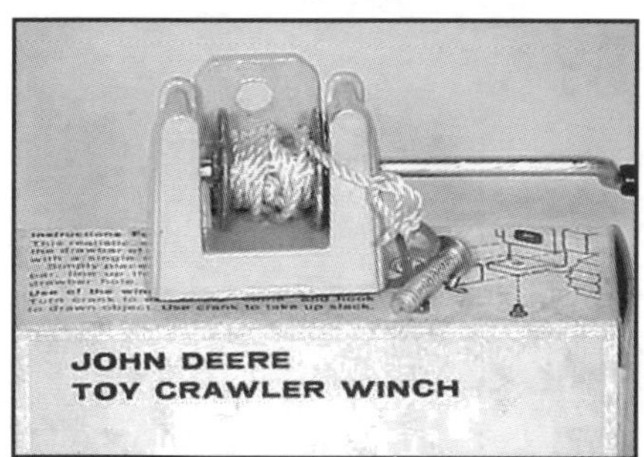

□ Winch. 1966, Ertl, Die, Accessory For JD-450 Crawler, 551, Excellent-NIB $20-35
Notes:

□ MC, 1995, SpecCast, Die, Crawler, Plow City Show, Cust 365, NIB $48
Notes:

□ MC, 1996, SpecCast, Die, Crawler, With Blade, Green Ag Model, JDM096, Excellent-NIB $25-35
□ ALSO SAME, Except "FFA Millennium," NIB $50
□ ALSO SAME, Except "CE Lake Region 12th Annual, NIB $50
Notes:

□ MC, 1996, SpecCast, Die, Industrial Yellow Model, JDM076, Excellent-NIB $25-35
Notes:

□ MI, 1997, SpecCast, Die, Industrial Tractor, Special Edition, JDM113, NIB $32
Notes:

□ Skid Steer Loader, 1981, Ertl, Die, Yellow, 571, NIB $30
Notes:

□ Skid Steer Loader, 1986, Ertl, Die, Yellw, 554EO, Exc-NIB $16-22
□ ALSO SAME, But More Detail, 554DO, Excellent-NIB $16-22
Notes:

□ Skid Steer Loader, 2000, Ertl, Die, Model 250, TBE15011, Excellent-NIB $20-25
Notes:

□ Trailer, 1990, Ertl, Die, Machine Trailer, Tandem Axle, Adjustable Loading Ramp, 594DO, NIB $25
Notes:

□ 40, 1954, Ertl, Die, Crawler, Green, With Or Without Blade, Excellent-NIB $260-570
□ ALSO SAME, But Yellow (See Color Section), Exc-NIB $300-700
Notes:

□ 40, 1999, Ertl, Die, Crawler, Green, 5072, NIB $20
Notes:

□ 40, 1999, Ertl, Die, Crawler, "19th Annual Plow City Farm Show," 16010, NIB $55
□ ALSO SAME, Except No Inscription, NIB $24
Notes:

□ 420, 1956, Ertl, Die, Crawler, Green With Yellow Stripe, Excellent-NIB $325-650
Notes:

□ 420, 1998, Ertl, Die, Crawler, Collector Edition "18th Plow City Show 1998," NIB $55
Notes:

□ 420, 1998, Ertl, Die, Crawler, Collector Edition With Blade, 5067DA, NIB $40
Notes:

□ 420, Nolt, Custom, Tractor, Industrial, Yellow, By Stephan , $275
Notes:

□ 430, 1997, Ertl, Die, Crawler, Collector Ed, Green/Yellow, Red Gas Cap, 5941DA, NIB $47
Notes:

□ 430, 1997 Ertl Die, Crawler, Industrial Yellow, Black Exhaust, Standard Air Precleaner, 5771DO, NIB $20
Notes:

□ 430, 1997, Ertl, Die, Crawler, With Blade, "7th Annual Toy Truck & Construction Show," 481TA, NIB $47.

□ 430, 2000, Ertl, Die, Crawler, "20Th Annual Plow City Show 2000," NIB $60
Notes:

□ 430, 2000, Ertl, Die, Crawler, With Blade, Industrial Yellow, 15234, NIB $22
Notes:

□ 440, 1959, Ertl, Die, Crawler, Excellent-NIB $275-650
Notes:

□ 440, 1959, Ertl, Die, Tractor, 3 Point, Excellent-NIB $400-850
□ ALSO SAME, Except 1962, No 3 Point, Excellent-NIB $435-925
Notes:

□ 450, 1965, Ertl, Die, Crawler, With Levers, Bubble Box, 546, Excellent-NIB $120-295
Notes:

□ 450, 1967, Ertl, Die, Crawler, With Winch, Enclosed Box, 554, Excellent-NIB $125-350
Notes:

□ 450, 1973, Ertl, Die, Crawler, With ROPS, Black Seat, 509, NIB $150
□ ALSO SAME, Except 1975, Yellow Seat, 540, Exc-NIB $50-80
Notes:

□ 450, 1973, Ertl, Die, Crawler, With ROPS, Black Seat, And Winch, 509, NIB $150
Notes

☐ 450, 1979, Ertl, Die, Crawler, With ROPS, Yellow, Stock No. 521, NIB $80
Notes:

☐ 650H, 2002, Ertl/RC, Crawler, Precision #1, TBE15410, NIB $115
Notes:

☐ 730, 1994, Yoder, Plastic, Tractor, Industrial, NIB $75
Notes:

☐ 830, 1991, Stephan, Custom, Tractor, NIB $325
Notes:

☐ 1010, 1963, Ertl, Die, Crawler, Yellow, 526, Excell-NIB $450-900
ALSO SAME, Except Green, Rare, Excellent-NIB $1000-1800.
Notes:

☐ 1010, 1995, Stephan, Custom, Industrial Utility, Excellent Detail, NIB $275
Notes:

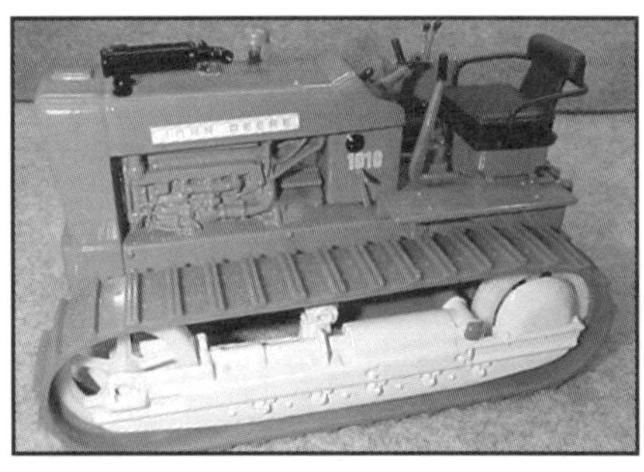

☐ 1010, 2001, Ertl/RC, Die, 1010 Crawler With Blade, Ag Version, 15191, NIB $30
Notes:

☐ 1010, 2001, Ertl/RC, Die, 1010 Crawler With Blade, Industrial Version, 15190A, NIB $45
Notes:

☐ 1010, Silver, NIB $1000
☐ ALSO SAME, Except Gold-Plated, NIB $800
Notes:

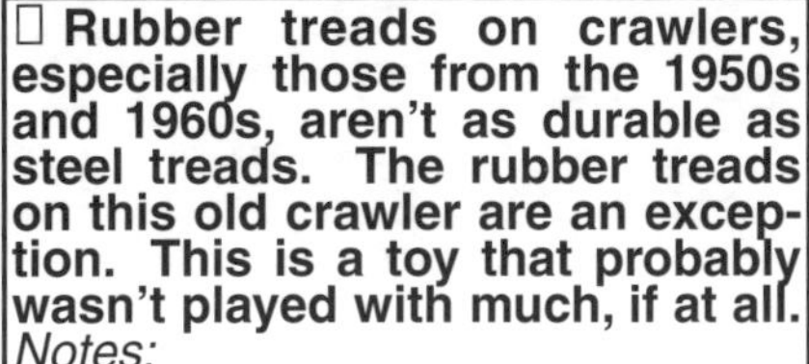

☐ Rubber treads on crawlers, especially those from the 1950s and 1960s, aren't as durable as steel treads. The rubber treads on this old crawler are an exception. This is a toy that probably wasn't played with much, if at all.
Notes:

☐ **1010, 2002, Ertl/RC, Die, Crawler, Metal Tracks And Ripper, "22nd Annual Plow City Farm Toy Show 2002," NIB $30** *Notes:*

☐ **1010, 2002, Ertl/RC, Die, Crawler, Ag Version, TBE15384, NIB $60**
Notes:

☐ **2755, 1991, Ertl, Die, Tractor, FWA With Loader & Cab, Yellow, 5677DO, Excellent-NIB $32-50**
Notes:

☐ **5010, 1989, Ertl, Die, Tractor, Industrial, Yellow, 5529DO, Excellent-NIB $40-60**
Notes:

☐ **9200, 1990s, Precision Engineering, Same As Regular 9200 Tractor, Except Yellow , NIB $185**
Notes:

☐ **9400, 2000, Precision Engineering Die, Custom, Industrial, NIB $185**
Notes:

☐ **Backhoe/Loader, 1975, Ertl, Plastic, Model 310, Kit, 8015, NIB $35**
Notes:

Begin 1/25 Scale

☐ **Backhoe/Loader, 1999, Ertl, Plastic, 310, Kit Reissue In New Box, 15043, NIB $17**
Notes:

☐ Excavator, 1971, Ertl, Die, Model 690, 505, Excell-NIB $50-75
Notes:

☐ Grader, 1971, Ertl, Die, 570, Crossbar Reinforced Or Not, 504, Excellent-NIB $35-70
☐ ALSO SAME, Except 502, In Black Box, Excellent-NIB $35-70
Notes:

☐ Scraper, 1971, Ertl,Die, Elevating Scraper, 860, W/ OR W/O ROPS, Windshield, Yellow, 506 Or 507, Excellent-NIB $150-275
☐ ALSO SAME, Except 1973, Ertl, W/ROPS, 508CO, Exc-NIB $100-150
Notes:

☐ Excavator, 690DLC, Hydraulic, NA
Notes:

☐ Wheel Loader, 1979, Ertl, Die, 644, ROPS, 507, Excell-NIB $25-38
☐ ALSO SAME, Except 1996, 644G, Revised, 507DP, NIB $25
Notes:

☐ Backhoe/Loader, 1994, Ertl, Die, Model 310D, 5520, NIB $25
Notes:

Begin 1/32 Scale

☐ Backhoe/Loader, 1994, Ertl, Die, Model 310D, Updated Graphics, 5520DO, NIB $25
Notes:

☐ Crawler, 1990, Ertl, Die, Model 550G, Blade, ROPS, Enclosed Engine, 5573DO, NIB $10
Notes:

☐ Log Skidder, 1991, Ertl, Die, 648E, ROPS, 5644, NIB $17
Notes:

☐ **Backhoe/Loader, 1991, SpecCast, Pewter, Model 310, JDM-011, NIB $25**
Notes:

Begin 1/43 Scale

(Photo Courtesy Of SpecCast)

☐ **Backhoe/Loader, 2000, SpecCast, Pewter, Model 310SE, JDM-097, NIB $25**
☐ **Backhoe-Loader, 2000, Spec, Pewter, 310SE, JDM110, NIB $35**
☐ **ALSO SAME, Except Stocking Holder, NIB $35**
Notes:

(Photo Courtesy Of SpecCast)

☐ **Crawler, 2000, Spec, Pewter, 850C, JDM142, NIB $30**
☐ **ALSO SAME, Except On Stocking Holder, (Shown Above,) NIB $30**
Notes:

(Photo Courtesy Of SpecCast)

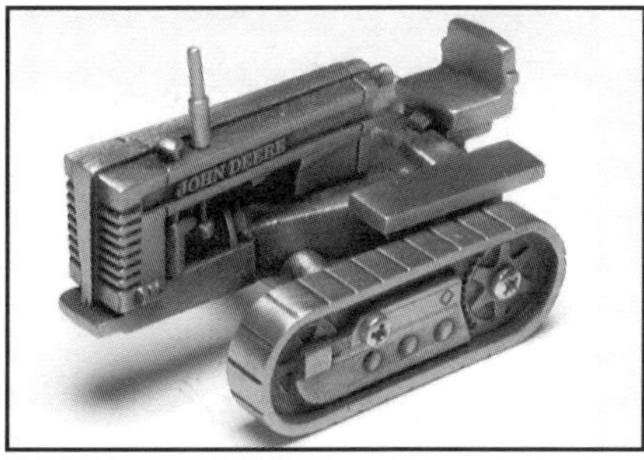

☐ **Crawler, MC, 1995, SpecCast, Pewter, JDM063, NIB $25**
☐ **ALSO SAME, Except "Achieving The Vision," Cust330, NIB $25**
Notes:

(Photo Courtesy Of SpecCast)

☐ **Crawler, 850, 1984, PPC, Pewter, With Blade And ROPS, NIB $25**
Notes:

☐ **Crawler, 850C, 1996, SpecCast, Die, Pewter, Crawler With Blade, JDM 084, NIB $35**
☐ **ALSO SAME, Except 1997, "Expo 97," JDM098, $35**
Notes:

(Photo Courtesy Of SpecCast)

☐ **Crawler, 850C, Ertl, Die, Rubber Tracks, Blade, Series II, 15232, NIB $10**
Notes:

☐ **Excavator, 690ELC, 1995, SpecCast, Pewter, NIB $30**
Notes:

(Photo Courtesy Of SpecCast)

☐ **Wheel Loder, 544B, 1984, PPC, Pewter, Underside Inscription: "John Deere Davenport Works," NIB $35**
Notes:

(Photo Courtesy Of SpecCast)

☐ Backhoe/Loader, 1997, Ertl, Die, 310SE, 5769EO, NIB $12
Notes:

Begin 1/50 Scale

☐ Backhoe/Loader, 2002, Ertl/RC, 310SG, TBE15231, NIB $30
Notes:

☐ Backhoe, 2001, SpecCast, Pewter, 310G, JDM 168, NIB $25
☐ ALSO SAME, Except Part Of Pen Set, NIB $30
Notes:

(Photo Courtesy Of SpecCast)

☐ Crawler, 1996, Ertl, Die, Model 850C, 5261EO, NIB $18
Notes:

☐ Crawler, 2002, SpecCast, Pewter, 450H, JDM138, NIB $28
Notes:

(Photo Courtesy Of SpecCast)

☐ Excavator, 200LC, 1997, Ertl, Die, Hydraulic 5260EO, NIB $15
Notes:

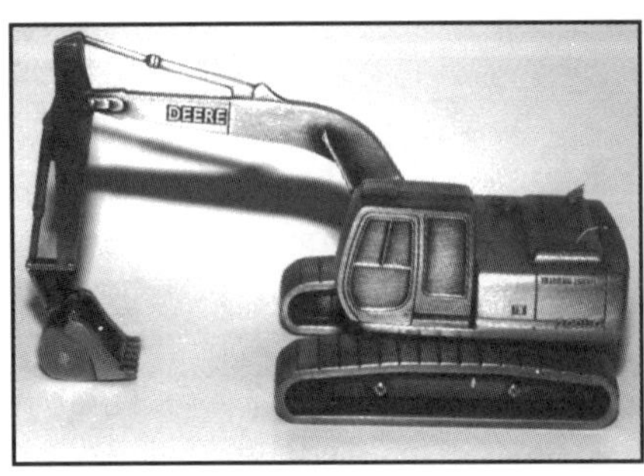

☐ Excavator, 2002, SpecCast, Pewter, 200LC, JDM152, NIB $30
Notes:

☐ Fork Lift, SpecCast, Pewter, JDM154, NIB $25
Notes:

☐ Grader, 772CH, 1999, Ertl, Die, 15039, NIB $18
Notes:

☐ **Skid Steer Loader, SpecCast, Pewter, Model 250, NIB $18**
Notes:

☐ **Wheel Loader, 744H, 1998, Ertl, Die, 5085EO, NIB $35**
Notes:

☐ **Wheel Loader, 744H, SpecCast, Pewter, JDM-101, NIB $35**
☐ **ALSO SAME, Except With Pen Set, JDM-103, NIB $40**
Notes:

(Photo Courtesy Of SpecCast)

☐ **Backhoe-Loader, 1984, Ertl, Die, 310D, 5521EO, NIB $10**
Notes:

Begin 1/64 Scale

☐ **Backhoe-Loader, 1994, ED, 310D, Updated Graphics, 5521EP, NIB $7**
Notes:

☐ **Bulldozer, 1995, Ertl, Die, 450D, 568EP, NIB $7**
Notes:

☐ **Crawler, 1985, Ertl, Die, With Blade, ROPS, Yellow, 568EO, NIB $7**
Notes:

☐ **Crawler, 1996, Ertl, Die, Green, 5616EO, NIB $5**
Notes:

☐ **Crawler, 2000, Ertl, 430, Crawler On Furrow Magazine Card, 15156, NIB $6** *Notes:*

□ Crawler, 2000, Ertl, Die, 430 Model, "20th Annual Plow City Show," Part Of 1/16 & 1/64 Set, Green & Yellow, NA
□ ALSO SAME, Except Gold Color, NIB $60
Notes:

□ Excavator, 1986, Ertl, Die, 690C, Tracked, 579FO, NIB $8
□ Excavator, 1994, Ertl, Die, 680D LC, Updated Graphics, 579FP, NIB $8
Notes:

□ Excavator, 1995, Ertl, Die, 579EO, NIB $8
Notes:

□ Grader, 1987, Ertl, Die, 772B, Industrial Yellow, 5540EO, NIB $5
□ ALSO SAME, Except 1995, 772BH, 5540, NIB $5
□ ALSO SAME, Except 1997, Revised Graphics, 5540EP, NIB $5
Notes:

□ MI, 1995, Ertl, Die, Orange, Part Of History Set 5523ER, NIB $3
Notes:

□ Skid-Steer Loader, 1989, Ertl, Die, 675, With Locking Arms & Bucket, 5536EO, NIB $7
Notes:

□ Skid-Steer Loader, 1997, Ertl, Die, 6675, Industrial, 5925EO, NIB $5
Notes:

□ Wheel Loader, 1988, Ertl, Die, 554G, Wheel Loader, 5539CO, NIB $7
□ ALSO SAME, Except 1994, Updated Graphics, 5539EP, NIB $7
□ ALSO SAME, Except 544E, NIB $7
Notes:

□ Backhoe-Loader, 2000, Ertl, Die, Model 310SE, TBE 33511, NIB $7
Notes:

Begin 1/87 Scale

☐ Gator, 2001, Ertl/RC, Die, 6 x 4, 15278, NA
Notes:

Begin 1/16 Scale

☐ Gator, 2001, Ertl/RC, Battery-Operated 4x2 Gator, TBEK15181, NA
Notes:

☐ 110, Ertl, Die, With Cart, And In Rare Brown Box, NIB $550
Notes:

☐ 110, 1965, Ertl, Die, With Cart, In Bubble Box, 543, NIB $$450
Notes:

☐ 110, 1967, Ertl, Die, Without "110" Decals, Excell-NIB $75-220
Notes:

☐ 110, 2001, Ertl/RC, Die, Precision Classic, 15213, NIB $45
Notes:

☐ 140, 1967, Ertl, Die, Comes In Green Square Box, Metal Steering Wheel, NIB $165
Notes:

☐ 140, 1968, Ertl, Die, Variations, 550, Excellent-NIB $85-155
☐ ALSO SAME, Except Plastic Steering Wheel, Other Variations, 550, Excellent-NIB $70-125
Notes:

☐ 140, 1976, Ertl, Die, Maintenance Set, 580, Excellent-NIB $400-800
Notes:

☐ 140, 1969, Ertl, Die, Color set, With Display, Exc-NIB $2000-3500
☐ ALSO SAME, Individual Tractors W/ Decal And Other Variations, Patio Red (See Color Plates), Sunset Orange, Spruce Blue, And April Yellow, Each, Excellent-NIB $300-400
Notes:

☐ 140, 1974, Ertl, Die, With Blade And Cart, Variations, 515, Excellent-NIB $125-275
Notes:

☐ 200 Series, 1988, Ertl, Die, 5591EO, Excellent-NIB $25-35
Notes:

☐ 200 Series, 1988, Ertl, Die, With Cart, 5594EO, Excell-NIB $25-35
Notes:

☐ 300, Ertl, Die, With Blade And Cart, 515, Rare With Box, Excellent-NIB $65-250
Notes:

☐ 300, Ertl, Die, With Trailer, 598, Excellent-NIB $25-65
Notes:

☐ 300, Ertl, Die, 591, NIB $40
Notes:

☐ 325, (Also Called "400",) 2001, Ertl/RC, Die, With Tiller And Dump Cart, 15199, NIB $15
☐ ALSO SAME, Except Ag Tires, Mower And Dump Cart, NIB $15
Notes:

☐ 345, 1997, Ertl, Die, With Mower Deck, Snow Blower, & Blade, 5079DO, Excellent-NIB $12-15
Notes:

☐ **400, 1978, Ertl, Die, With Large Strobe Decal, 591, Excellent-NIB $22-35**
Notes:

☐ **400, (Also Called "300" Series,) 1978, Ertl, Die, No Strobe On Decal, 591, NIB $40**
Notes:

☐ **400, (Also Called "317" or "318",) 1985, Ertl, Die, Lawn & Garden, Small Strobe Decal, 591EO, Excellent-NIB $22-35**
Notes:

☐ **400, 1987, Ertl, Die, Lawn & Garden, Small Strobe Decal, W/Cart, 598EO, Excellent-NIB $22-40**
Notes:

☐ **425, 2002, Ertl, Die, L&G Tractor With Snow Blower And Mower, 5749, NIB $15**
Notes:

☐ **600, 1988, Ertl, Die, AMT (All Materials Transport), With Dump Bed, 5597DO, NIB $18**
Notes:

☐ **4310, 2002, Ertl/RC, Die, L&G Tractor With Attachments, TBE15198, NIB $25**
Notes:

☐ **SST18, 2001, Ertl/RC, Die, Spinsteer With Mower, 15292, NIB $15**
Notes:

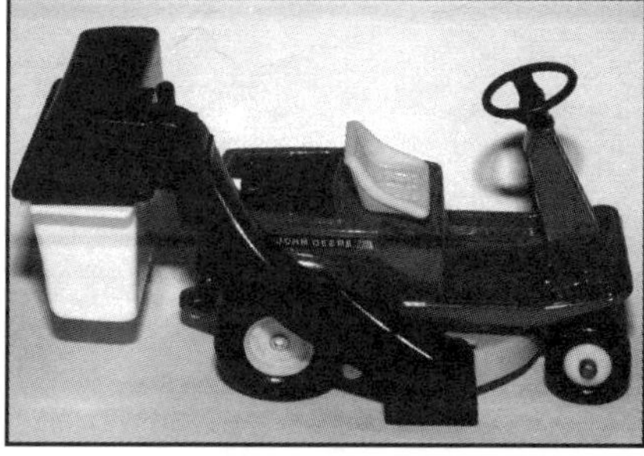

☐ **RX75, 1990, Ertl, Die, Rear bagger, 5588EO, 1/12 Scale, NIB $118**
Notes:

☐ Gator, 2000, Ertl, Die, Assorted Colors, TBE36161, NIB $18
☐ Gator, 1996, SpecCast, Die, Pewter, 4 x 6, JDMO80, NIB $18
☐ Gator, 2001, Ertl/RC, Die, 6 x 4, World of Opportunity--JD Expo 2001--San Antonio, 15289A, NIB $20

Begin 1/32 Scale

☐ Z-Trak, 1999, Ertl, Die, Lawn Mower, 15018, NIB $12
Notes:

☐ 425, 1995, Ertl, Die, With Removable Mower Deck & Snow Blade, 5740EO , NIB $8
Notes:

☐ 325, SpecCast, Pewter, JDM-100, NIB $20
Notes:

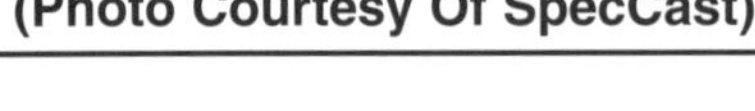

(Photo Courtesy Of SpecCast)

☐ 425, 1995, Ertl, Die, With Snowblower & Mower, 5745EO, NIB $15
Notes:

☐ 445, 1995, Ertl, Die, With Snowblower & Mower, 5741EO, NIB $8
Notes:

☐ 455, 1995, Ertl, Die, With Tiller & Mower, 5742EO, NIP $8
Notes:

☐ 1445, 2001, SpecCast, Pewter, Lawn Machine, JDM166, NIB $20
Notes:

☐ 110, 1994, SpecCast, With Mower & Deck JDM070, NIB $20
☐ ALSO SAME, Except 1995, Custom, "John Deere Horicon Works," Scale, NIB $25
Notes:

Begin 1/43 Scale

☐ **425, Plastic, Lawn & Garden Tractor, Green & Yellow, NIB $4**
Notes:

Begin 1/64 Scale

☐ **445, Plastic, Lawn & Garden Tractor, Green & Yellow, NIB $4**
Notes:

☐ **455, Plastic, Lawn & Garden Tractor, Green & Yellow, NIB $4**
Notes:

☐ **Gator, 2003, Ertl/RC, Die & Plastic, Worksite, Plastic Chassis With Working Metal Dump Box, 1/16, TBE15516, NIB $15**
Notes:

Various Gators

☐ **Gator, 2004, Ertl/RC, Die, CX Compact Gator, 1/16, TBE15637, NA**

☐ **Gator, 2004, Ertl/RC, Die, HPX 4x4, 1/16, TBE15636, NA**

☐ **Gator, 2003, Ertl/RC, Die, 6x4, New Graphics, Free-Rolling Rubber Wheels, Working Dump Box, 1/32, TBE15254, NIB $6**
Notes:

☐ **Gator, 2004, Ertl/RC, Die, HPX 4x4, 1/32, TBE15692, NA**

☐ **Gator, 2002, Ertl/RC, Plastic, 3", TBEK15411, NA**

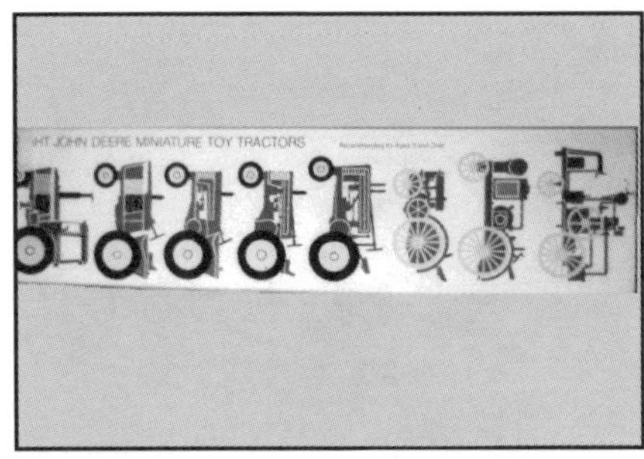

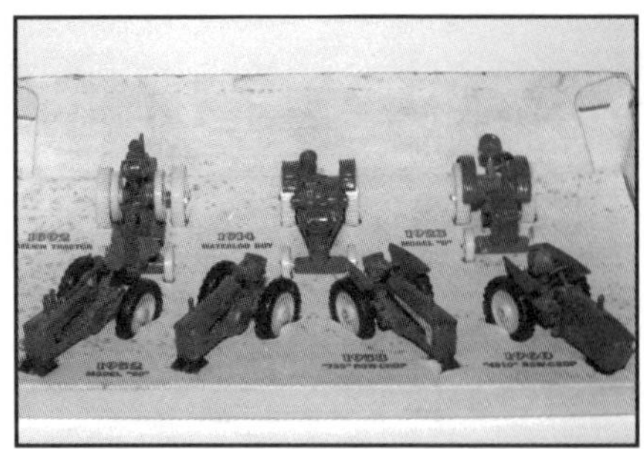

□ 1960, Ertl, Die, Milestones Set, 7 Pieces, White Horizontal Card, Variations, 1/64 Scale, NIP $200.
Notes:

□ 1960, Ertl, Die, Historical Set, 7 Individually Boxed Tractors, With Hooks, 1/64 Scale, 560, NIB $65
□ ALSO SAME, Except 1972, And 8 Boxed Tractors, With Hooks, NIB $60
□ ALSO SAME, Except 1985, 593, No Hooks, (Shown Above)NIB $50
Notes:

1960, Ertl, Die, Milestones Historical Set, 7 Pieces, Open Box Covered With Plastic Wrap, 1/64 Scale, NIB $275
Notes:

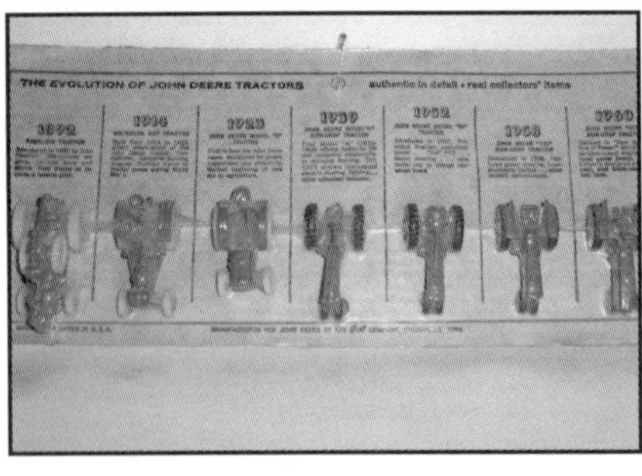

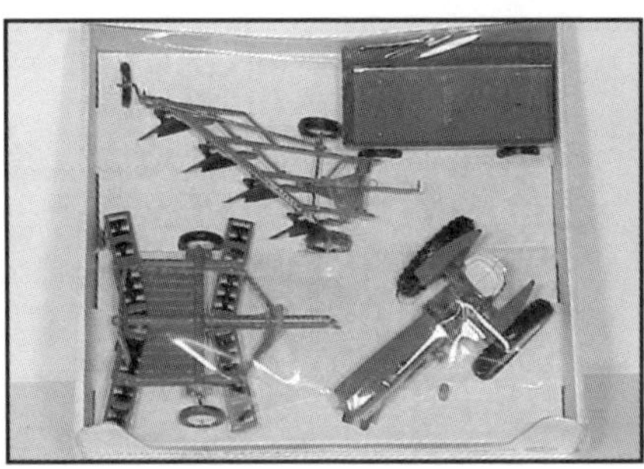

□ 1967, Ertl, Die, 7 Piece Evolution of John Deere Set, Plain White Blister Pack, 1/64 Scale, With Plastic Fenders, NIP $125
□ ALSO SAME, Except Metal Fenders, NIP $225
Notes:

□ 1969, Ertl, Die, 3020 With Disc And Plow, 1/16 Scale, 536, NIB $475
Notes:

□ 1969, Ertl, Die, 3020 With Flare Box Wagon In Closed Box, 1/16 Scale, NIB $400
□ ALSO SAME, Except Also With Disc And Plow, 536, NIB $475
Notes:

□ 1973, Ertl, Die, 4430, Disc, Plow, Flare Box Wagon, Shed Box, 1/16 Scale, 514, NIB $295
Notes:

□ 1977, Ertl, Die, 2030 Solid Stripe Tractor With Barge Wagon, 518, 1/16 Scale, NIB $60
Notes:

□ 1979, Ertl, Die, 8640 With Black Frame Fold-Over Disc, 1/16 Scale, 599, NIB $220
□ ALSO SAME, Except 1975, 8630 With Yellow Frame Fold Over Disc, 599, NIB $275
Notes:

☐ **1979, Ertl, Die, 4440 With Strobe Stripe, And Barge Wagon, 518,1/32 Scale, NIB $28**
Notes:

☐ **1979, Ertl, Die, 4430 Narrow Front With Barge Wagon, 70, 1/32 Scale, NIB $15**
☐ **ALSO SAME, Except 2001, Reintroduction of 1979 Set, TBE70, NIB $15**
Notes:

☐ **1982, Ertl, Die, 4450 W/Skid Loader & Barge Wagon, Shed Box, 1/16 Scale, 502, NIB $140**
Notes:

☐ **1982, Ertl, Die, 8650 With Black Frame Fold Over Disc, 1/16 Scale, 5510, NIB $185**
Notes:

☐ **1983, Ertl, Die, 2550 With Barge Wagon, 5511, 1/32 Scale, NIB $35**
Notes:

☐ **1986, Ertl, Die, 4250 W/Forage Harvester & Forage Wagon, 553, NIB $140**
Notes:

☐ **1986, Ertl, Die, Mini 4 Piece Farm Set, Anhydrous Ammonia Tank, Gravity Feed Wagon, Sprayer, Tractor, 5518EO, 1/64 Scale, NIB $20**
Notes:

☐ **1986, Ertl, Die, Mini 6 Piece Farm Set, Tractor, Trailer With Endloader, Wagon, Round Baler, Forage Wagon, Forage Harvester, 5514EO, 1/64 Scale, NIB $25**
Notes:

☐ **1987, Ertl, Die, 150th Anniversary Desk Set: Waterloo Boy, 440, Plow, 110 LGT, 50 Series, 1/64 Scale, 5519, NIB $30**
Notes:

□ 1988, Ertl, Die, Historical Set Of 4 Pieces: Waterloo Boy, G, M, R, Bubble Pack, 5523,1/64 Scale, NIB $10
□ ALSO SAME, Except 1989, More Detail On R On Rubber Tires, Bubble Pack, 5523EO, NIB $10
Notes:

□ 1989, Ertl, Die, Unstyled "A" With Flare Box Wagon, 1/16 Scale, 5541, NIB $30
Notes:

□ 1989, Ertl, Die, Battery Operated Set: Tractor With PTO Dump Box Wagon, 1/32 Scale, 5624DO, NIB $40
Notes:

□ 1990, Ertl, Die, Unstyled A's, 1/43 & 1/16 Unstyled "A"'S, 5632, NIB $30
Notes:

□ 1991, Ertl, Die, 3 Piece Micro Set, 60 Series Tractor, Wagon, Disk, 1/128 Scale, 5572FO, NIB $5
Notes:

□ 1992, Ertl, Die, Four Piece Pillsbury Canada Set: Tractor, Plow, Disc, Wagon, "Green Giant" On Hood & Wagon Sides; Some With English And French (Two Versions), 4913CO, 1/16 Scale, Often Not Considered JD, NA
Notes:

□ 1992, Ertl, Die, 630 LP And D Tractors, 5685EO, 1/64 Scale, NIB $8
Notes:

□ 1994, Ertl, Die, Tractor And Implement Set, 5673, 1/32 Scale, NIB $15
Notes:

□ 1994 Ertl, Die, Tractor, Baler And Rake, 5747, 1/64 Scale, NIB $12
Notes:

☐ 1995, Ertl, Die, Haymaking Set Of 7800 Tractor And 4 Pieces, 1/64 Scale, 5626DR, NIB $20
Notes:

☐ 1995, Ertl, Die, 50 Series, Set 1, 50 WF, 520 WF, 530 NF, 5262EO,1/64 Scale, NIB $25
Notes:

☐ 1995, Ertl, Die, Construction Set: 310D, 690DLC & 648E, 5841EO, 1/64 Scale, NIB $18
Notes:

☐ TOP: 1995, Ertl, D, Set: Overtime, 80, Unstyled G, MI, 5523ER, 1/64 Scale, NIB $12
Notes:

☐ 1995, Ertl, Die, 70 With Rake, 5807DO, 1/16 Scale, NIB $30
Notes:

☐ 1996, Ertl, Die, 1931 Model GP Standard Tractor On Steel And Flarebox Wagon, 5062, 1/16 Scale, NIB $30
Notes:

☐ 1996, Ertl, Cold Cast Porcelain, "Lowell Davis America," "Sooie," Tractor With Flare Box Wagon On Plaque, Snow, 2521AO, NIB $20
Notes:

☐ 1997, Ertl, Die, Set No. 3, 50 NF, 520 WF, 530 Adjustable WF, 5854, 1/64 Scale, NIB $25
Notes:

☐ 1998, Ertl, Die, 5020 Yellow Industrial Tractor With Disc, TBE-5198, 1/64 Scale, NIP $8
Notes:

□ 1999, Ertl, Die, 60 Series Historical Set: 60 RC, 620 Wheatland, 620WF, 5862EO, 1/64 Scale, NIP $15
Notes:

□ 2000, Ertl, Die, Construction Set With Wheel Loader, Crawler With Blade, Hydraulic Excavator, Tractor Backhoe Loader, Motor Grader, Implement Trailer and Pickup, TBE36310, 1/64 Scale, NIP $7 Each
Notes:

□ 2000, Ertl, Die, Harvesting Set With Model 95 Combine, 2510 Tractor, Flare Wagon, Chevy Grain Truck, TBE15014, 1/64 Scale, NIP $15
Notes:

□ 2000, Ertl, Die, 5 Pieces, Harvesting Set, W/8410 Tractor, Wing Disc, Sprayer, Manure Tanker, Fertilizer Spreader, TBE15079, NIP $12
Notes:

□ 2000, Implement Set, With Manure Spreader, Soil Saver, Rotary Chopper, Mower Conditioner, TBE5959 0, 1/64 Scale, NIB $16
Notes:

□ 2000, Ertl, Die, 2440 With Wagon, TBE15164, 1/16 Scale, NIB $25
Notes

□ 2000, Ertl, Die, Assortment, Wagons: Auger, Hay, Flare, Bale, & Implement Trailer & Hydra-Push Spreader, TBE36233, 1/64 Scale, NIB $10
Notes:

□ 2000, Ertl, Die, Vintage Set: Waterloo Boy, D Styled, R, 5020, TBE36234 , 1/64 Scale, NIB $6 Each
Notes:

□ 2000, Ertl, Die, Construction Set W/ Wheel Loader, Hydraulic Excavator, Crawler w/Blade, Tractor Backhoe Loader, TBE2342, 1/50, Scale, NIB $20
Notes:

□ 2000, Ertl, Porcelain, John Deere Tractor, "Winter Calf," 5102, 1/16 Scale, NIB $20
Notes:

□ 2001, Ertl/RC, Die, 630 NF With Mounted Corn Picker & Flare Box Wagon, 15086, 1/64, Scale, NIB $10
Notes:

□ 2001, Ertl/RC, Die, 7610 Tractor With Grain Cart, 15221, 1/64 Scale, NIB $10
Notes:

□ 2001, Ertl/RC, Die, Lawn & Grounds Care Assortment, Gator, L&G Tractor, Front Mower, 36518, 1/16 Scale, NIB $8 Each

Notes:

□ 2001, Ertl/RC, Die, 4 Pieces, 4620, 4010, 4020, 4320 Tractors, TBE15216, NIP $18
Notes:

□ 2001, Ertl/RC, Die, 3 Pieces, Styled B, Styled G, Styled H, TBE15217, 1/64 Scale, NIB $13
Notes:

□ 2001, Ertl/RC, Die, 4WD 9400, 4WD 8870, 36481, 1/64 Scale, NA
Notes:

□ 2002, Ertl/RC, Die, 3 Pieces, Tracked Tractor, Tillage Implements, TBE15375, 1/64 Scale, NIP $18
Notes:

□ 2002, Ertl/RC, Die, 4010 Tractor With Mounted Corn Picker & Barge Wagon, TBE15377, NIB $10
Notes:

☐ **2002, Ertl/RC, Die, 3350 Trac-tor With Model 100 Square Baler, TBE15369, NIB $22**
Notes:

☐ **2002, Ertl/RC, Die, 6410 Trac-tor With 590 Round Baler, TBE-15370, NIB $22**
Notes:

☐ **2002, Ertl/RC, Die, Farm Toy Playset, Variety Of Tractors And Implements, Pickups, Trailer, Barn, 75 Pieces, 15398, 1/64 Scale, NIP $40**
Notes:

☐ **2002, Ertl/RC, Die, Farm Toy Playset, Assorted Tractors And Implements, And Farm Items, 75 Pieces, 15456, 1/64 Scale, NIP $40**
Notes:

☐ **2002, Ertl, Die, 3020 Tractor With Duals On Left Side Only, And 4-Bottom Plow, 15076, 1/16 Scale, NIB $28**
Notes:

☐ **2003, Ertl/RC, Die, 6210/Loader and Manure Spreader, 1/32, TBE15488, NA**
Notes:

☐ **2003, Ertl/RC, Die, 6410/Wagon and Disc Set, 1/32, TBE15489, NA**
Notes:

☐ **2003, Ertl/RC, Die, Haying: Tractor, Mower Conditioner, Hay Rake and Baler, 1/64, TBE15497, NA**
Notes:

☐ **2003, Ertl/RC, Die, Vintage Tractor, Wagon And Skid-Steer Assortment, 1/16, TBEK37010, NA**
Notes:

☐ **2004, Ertl/RC, Die, 5-Piece Value Set: Tractor, Gator, Tank, Injector & Trailer, 1/64, TBE37087, NA**
Notes:

☐ **2004, Ertl/RC, Die, 4430, 4440, 4450, 1/16, No. 15492, NA**
Notes:

☐ **Ertl, Die, D And Flare Wagon, 50620NIB $28**
Notes:

☐ **Ertl, Die, 2-Piece Set, "Special Waterloo Edition," Limited Edition, 4000 Made, "John Deere Waterloo Operations," Waterloo Boy, 9400T Tractors, 15335, 1/64 Scale, NIB $35**
Notes:

☐ **Ertl, Die, Accessory Set: Post-Hole Digger, Bale Fork, Hog Carrier, 1/64 Scale, NIP $5**
Notes:

☐ **2440 Utility Tractor With Rear Blade & Bale Mover w/Bale, 15417, 1/16 Scale, NIB $15**
Notes:

☐ **Ertl, Die, 2440 Utility Tractor W/ Machine Trailer, 15418, 1/16 Scale, NIB $18**
Notes:

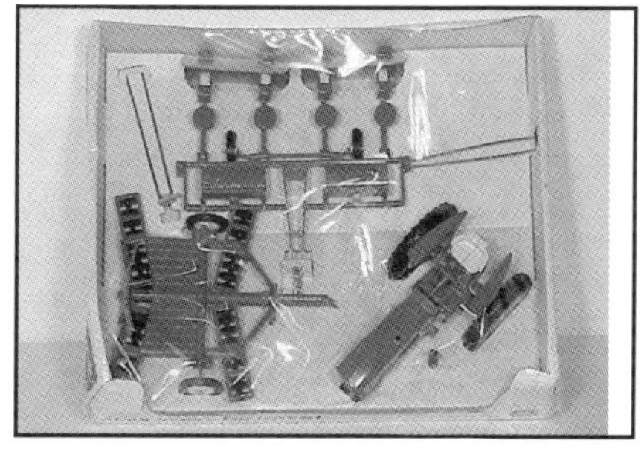

☐ **Ertl, 1960s, Die, Set, 3 Pieces, 3010 Tractor, Planter, Disc, 544, 1/16 Scale, NIB $495**
Notes:

☐ **Ertl, Die, Set, 4WD Tractor, Planter, Mulch Tiller, 5805, 1/64 Scale, NIP $20**
Notes:

☐ GMC Dealer Tiltbed Truck, 1977, Ertl, Die, GMC Flat Tiltbed Truck With Wheel Crank Winch, White, JD Logo On Truck Door, 1/16 Scale, 594, Exc-NIB $85-150
☐ ALSO SAME, Except 1980, Squared Bumper, Larger JD Logo On Door, Plastic Grille, 594, 1/16 Scale, Excellent-NIB $85-150
Notes:

☐ Chevrolet Blazer, 1982, Ertl, SS, Dealer Pickup, 3827, 1/64 Scale, NIB $20
Notes:

☐ Chevrolet Titan Parts Express, 1982, Ertl, SS, Semi-Tractor With Van Trailer, Varieties, 1/25 Scale, 5533, NIB $30
Notes:

☐ GMC Dealer Pickup, 1984, Ertl, SS, Individual Dealer Logos Available, Sunroof, "Nothing Runs Like A Deer," Various Decals, 543DO Or 5531, 1/16 Scale, NIB $16
Notes:

☐ International Equipment Hauler, 1987, Ertl, Die, Tandem Axle Straight Truck With Flat Bed, 1/64 Scale, 5542EO, NIB $7
Notes:

☐ International Grain Truck/Pup, 1987, Ertl, Die, Tandem Axle Straight Grain Truck With Tandem Axle Grain Trailer, 1/64 Scale, 5543EO, NIB $30
Notes:

☐ International Fertilizer Truck, 1987, Ertl, Die, Tandem Axle Straight Fertilizer Spreader Truck, 1/64 Scale, 5544EO, NIB $8
Notes:

☐ International Milk Truck, 1987, Ertl, Die, Tandem Axle Straight Milk Truck, 1/64 Scale, 5545EO, NIB $8
Notes:

☐ International Parts Express, 1987, Ertl, Die, Navistar Semi-Tractor With Van Trailer, 1/64 Scale, 5535EO, NIB $15
Notes:

☐ **Mack Bulldog Bank, 1987, Ertl, Die, Antique Mack Van Truck, "102" On Sides, 1/25 Scale, 5534EO, Excellent-NIB $25-65**
☐ **ALSO SAME, Except "103" On Sides, Excellent-NIB $10-15**
Notes:

☐ **1989, Ertl, Die, Four Piece Grain Set: Grain Truck, Grain Auger, Gravity Feed Wagon, Tractor, 5566DO, NIB $25**
Notes:

☐ **1989, Ertl, Die, Four Piece Fertilizer Set: Fertilizer Truck, Plow, Spreader, Tractor, 5567DO, NIB $25**
Notes:

☐ **Dain Stake Truck, 1990, Murphy, Die, Low Side Stake Truck, "John Deere Parts Express," Color Variations, 1/20 Scale, DSO249, Green NIB $15**
☐ **ALSO SAME, Except Gold-Plated, DASAT1561, NIB $65**
Notes:

☐ **Panel Bank, 1950 Chevy, 1990, Ertl, Die, Panel Truck With JD Logo, Bank, Green And White, Or Closed Brown Box, 5621EO, 1/25 Scalc, NIB $18**
Notes:

☐ **Truck, 1990, Pewter, SpecCast, Dain, 1/43 Scale, NIB $18**
Notes:

☐ **International Equipment Hauler, 1991, Ertl, Die, Navistar Semi-Tractor With Drop Deck Trailer And Two Tractors With Front Weights, Semi Has Wide Logo Stripe, 1/64 Scale, 5530EO, NIB $30**
Notes:

☐ **International S Log Truck, 1992, Ertl, SS, Semi Tractor With Log Trailer, Varieties, 1/25 Scale, 3180, NIB $35**
Notes:

☐ **Mack Bulldog Bank, 1992, Ertl, Die, Antique Mack Van Truck, "John Deere Customer Driven--Outside Parts Sales--Nashville 1992," Bank, Serial No, 1/25 Scale, "103" On Outside, 5564, NIB $35**
Notes:

☐ **Ford Pickup And Machine Trailer, 1992, Ertl, Die, Four Wheel Drive With Tandem Axle Machine Trailer, 5691, 1/64, NIB $8**
Notes:

☐ **1955 Chevy Cameo Bank, 1992, Ertl, Die, Pickup Truck With Crate Load, Bank, JD Logo On Doors, 5614EO, NIB $12**
Notes:

☐ **Ford Pickup/Livestock Trailer, 1992, Ertl, Die, Four-Wheel-Drive With Tandem Axle Livestock Trailer, 5712, 1/64, NIB $7**
Notes:

☐ **1931 Hawkeye Truck, 1994, Ertl, Die, With Model R Waterloo Boy On Back, 5768DO, 1/32 Scale, NIB $16**
Notes:

☐ **Peterbilt Semi With 7800 Tractors, 1995, Ertl, Die, 5831EO, 1/64 Scale, NIB $25**
Notes:

☐ **Chevy Dealer Delivery Truck With Model G, 1995, Ertl, Die, 5933EO, NIP $10**
Notes:

☐ **1996, Ertl, Die, JD Dealership Ford Pickup, Trailer & Skid Steer Loader, 5923, 1/32 Scale, NIB $20**
Notes:

☐ **1996, Peterbilt Truck And Flatbed Trailer With Two 7710 Tractors, Truck Doors Have JD Logo On Both Sides, 5207EO, NIB $23**
Notes:

☐ **1996, Ertl, Die, GMC Pickup With A JD Tractor On Trailer, 5924, NIB $10**
Notes:

☐ Diamond T Lube Express Truck, 1996, Ertl, Die, #109 In Bank Series, 5757DO, NIB $15
Notes:

☐ 1950 Chevy Prestige Bank, 1996, Ertl, Die, 5944CO, 1/25 Scale, NIB $30
Notes:

☐ 1950 Chevy Dealership Pickup, 1996, Ertl, Die, Bullnose Styling, 5936FO, 1/25 Scale, NIB $25
Notes:

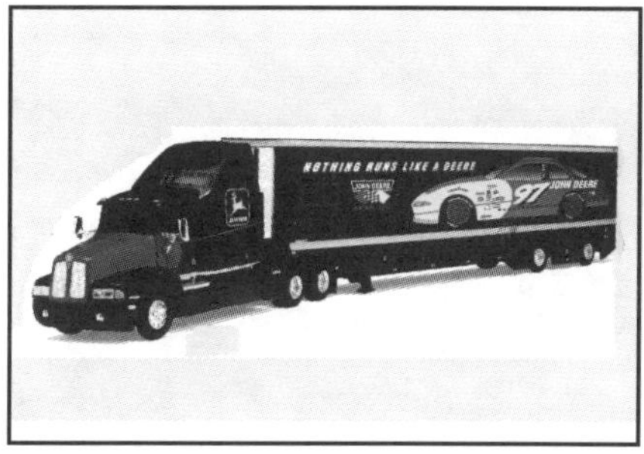

☐ Kenworth T600B Transporter, 1997, Ertl, Die, On Walnut Base, 5723AA, 1/43 Scale, NIB $135
Notes:

☐ John Deere Lawn & Garden Semi, 1997, 5032EO, NIB $13
Notes:

☐ Semi And Trailer, 1997, Ertl, Die, 50th Anniversary, Maximizer Combine, 1/64 Scale, 5127DA, NIB $28
Notes:

☐ 1957 Chevy Stake Truck, 1997, Ertl, Die, Prestige, 5049CO, 1/25 Scale, NIB $25
Notes:

☐ 1923 Chevy Van Bank, 1997, Ertl, Die, Bank, 5835DO, NIB $15
Notes:

☐ Construction Hauling Set, 1997, Ertl, Die, Backhoe-Loader, Revised, PM5574EP, NIB $25
Notes:

□ 1918 Model T Pickup Bank, 1997, Ertl, Die, "Merry Christmas 1997," 5135TO , NIB $15
Notes:

□ 1948 Diamond T Semi With Van Trailer, 1997, Ertl, Die, HO Scale, 5401DO, NIB $23
Notes:

□ 1940 Ford Pickup, 1998, Ertl, Die, Prestige Series, "Quality Parts, Quality Service," 5054DO, NIB $28
Notes:

□ 1998, Ertl, Die, 1960 Mack B-61 Semi And Flatbed Trailer, 2 JD 5020 Tractors, 5934EO, 1/64 Scale, NIB $16
Notes:

□ 1938 Chevrolet Delivery Truck, 1998, Ertl, Die, Bank, "Merry Christmas 1998," 15044, NIB $15
Notes:

□ 1948 Peterbilt Semi With 4020 Tractors, 1998, Ertl, Die, 5458CO, HO Scale, NIB $20
Notes:

□ Kenworth With Flatbed And 8300 Tractors, 1998, Ertl, Die, 5459CO, HO Scale, NIB $18
Notes:

□ Dodge Ram Dealership Pickup, 1998, Ertl, Die, 5097, 1/18 Scale, NIB $25
Notes:

□ Lawn Mowing Set, 1998, Ertl, Die, Pickup, Trailer, 455 L&G Tractor, 5009DO, NIB $18
Notes:

□ Ford F350 Pickup, 1999, Ertl, Die, 5076EO, 1/64 Scale, NIB $5
Notes:

□ 1947 Dodge Pickup, 1999, Ertl, Die, Prestige, "John Deere Parts & Service," 15024, NIB $27
Notes:

□ Semi, 2000, Ertl, Die, Parts Semi, 15023, 1/64 Scale, NIB $12
Notes:

□ Semi, 2000, Ertl/RC, Die, With John Deere Van Trailer, 5457CO, HO Scale, NIB $12
Notes:

□ Semi, 2000, Ertl/RC, Die, With Peterbilt Vintage John Deere Van Trailer, 5456CO, HO Scale, NIB $15
Notes:

□ Pickup, 2000, Ertl, Die, Ford Service Pickup, John Deere, TBE15091, NIB $22
Notes:

□ Semi, 2000, Ertl, Die, With Flat Trailer And 8310T & 8310 MFWD Tractors, TBE15078, 1/64 Scale, NIB $23
Notes:

□ 2000, Ertl, Die, Pickup, "John Deere Moline Ill" On Door, "Introducing The John Deere 'M' With Touch-o-matic" On Wood In Rear, 15092, NIB $22
Notes:

□ 2000, Ertl, Die, Semi W/Flat Trailer & Two 8310 Tractors TBE-15066, 1/87 Scale, NIB $18
Notes:

2000, Ertl, Die, F-350 Dealer Flatbed With 8410 tractor, TBE5799, 1/64 Scale, NIB $13
Notes:

☐ John Deere Panel Truck, 2001, Ertl, Die, No. 114 In Series, "Introducing G, The General Purpose Tractor," 15235, NIB $15
Notes:

☐ Pickup, 2001, Ertl/RC, Die, 1950 Chevy, Prestige, 15236, NIB $28
Notes:

☐ Dealership Pickup, 2001, Ertl, Die, With 6675 Skid-Steer Loader On Trailer, 5774EO, 1/64 Scale, NIB $10
Notes:

☐ Delivery Truck, 2001, Ertl/RC, Steel, Structor, John Deere 4440 Graphics, 15291, NIB $15
Notes:

☐ John Deere '53 Ford Delivery Truck Bank, Ertl, 2002, Die, Coin Slot Behind Rear Doors, #115 In Series, 15388, 1/25 scale, NIB $24
Notes:

☐ John Deere Gator 387 Peterbilt Semi, 2002, SpecCast, Die, New Style 387 Peterbilt, 33514, NIB $28
Notes:

☐ John Deere '57 Chevy Pickup, 2002, SpecCast, Die, Snowblower, Shovel, Oil Can, 1/25 Scale, 78038, NIB $30
Notes:

☐ 1957 Chevy Stake Truck, 2002, Ertl/RC, Die, With Mower, 78019, 1/25 scale, NIB $30
Notes:

☐ **Dealership Pickup, 2002, Ertl, Die, 15320, 1/64 Scale, NIB $4**
Notes:

☐ **John Deere 1946 Dodge Power Wagon, 2002, Ertl/RC, Die, Doors And Tailgate Open, Hood Raises, Tow Chain, 15389, 1/25 Scale, NIB $28**
Notes:

☐ **2002, Ertl, Die, Semi And Tractor, 15227, 1/64 Scale, NIB $25**
Notes:

☐ **Dealer Pickup, 2002, Ertl, Die, "John Deere Dealer Days," 1/64 Scale, 15293A, NIB $5**
Notes:

☐ **Truck, 2002, Ertl/RC, Die, 400D Articulated Dump Truck, 1/50, TBE15386, NIB $15**
Notes:

☐ **Chevy Flatbed Truck, Diecast Promotions, Die, Detailed Interior, Green, 50060, NIB $60 (Tractor Not Included)**
Notes:

☐ **Semi, Log Hauler, 5532DO, NIB $30**
Notes:

☐ **Dealer Pickup And Skid-Steer Loader, Ertl, Die, 5754, 1/64 Scale, NIB $10**
Notes:

☐ **Semi, Stepped Lowboy, Construction Hauling Set, Loader-Excavator On Back, 5570DO, 1/32 Scale, NIB $35**
Notes:

□ Pickup, "John Deere Parts & Service" On Wood In Back, "John Deere Moline Ill" On Door, NIB $24
Notes:

□ Semi, Side Of Trailer Says "The Right Choice...John Deere" 8000 and 8000T Series, 160 HP To 225 HP," 1/64 Scale, NIB $28
Notes:

□ Semi, Racing Car "97" On Side"Nothing Runs Like A Deere," 1/64 Scale, NIB $18
Notes:

□ Pickup, 20 Series Tractors, "Power Sizes And Types To Meet Every Farming Need," #113 In Series, 15091, NIB $22
Notes:

□ Pickup, Racing Type, "97" On Door, Various Advertising Elsewhere, NIB $18
Notes:

□ Panel Truck, Antique Type, "John Deere Moline Ill" On Door, "John Deere General Purpose Farm Tractors" On Panel, NIB $25
Notes:

□ Pickup, "Quality Farm Equipment" On Door, "John Deere Moline Ill USA" On Wood Side Of Pickup, NIB $28
Notes:

□ Ford F-150 Pickup, Ertl, Die, Sunroof, No. 5793, 1/16 Scale, NIB $15
Notes:

□ Kenworth Stake Truck, Bank, Antique, "Deere Company Moline Illinois" On Side, No. 108 On Door, NIB $13
Notes:

□ John Deere 97 Taurus Race Car, 2000, Ertl, Die, 7100, NA
Notes:

□ Race Car, 1997, Ertl, Die, 160th Anniversary Commemorative Race Car, 5183DA, 1/18 Scale, NIB $55
Notes:

□ □ 1930s Ford Roadster, 1998, Ertl, Die, Bank, 5050DO, 1/25th Scale, NIB $25
Notes:

□ Taurus Race Car, 1998, Ertl, Die, "97" On Door, 15000A, 1/18 Scale, NIB $50
□ ALSO SAME, Except Stock Car, Collector Edition, 15002A, 1/18 Scale, NIB $50
□ ALSO SAME, Except Walnut Base, NIB $125
Notes:

□ Mercury Chop Top Auto, 2002, Ertl/RC, Die, No. 8 In Racing Series, 96800-1, NIB $20
□ ALSO SAME, Except Gold, 98600-2, Both 1/24 Scale, NIB $35
Notes:

□ Taurus Stock Car, 1999, Ertl, Die, 15045, NIB $35
□ ALSO SAME, Except On Acrylic Base, 15049, NIB $35
□ ALSO SAME, Except On Walnut Base, 15049, NIB $125
Notes:

□ 1997 Pewter Car, SpecCast, NIB $35
Notes:

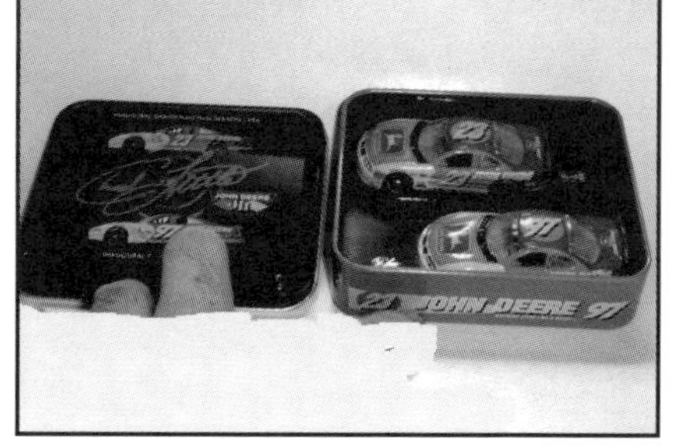

□ Tins Of Miniature Scale 1997 John Deere Racing Cars, NIB $15
Notes:

□ #23 Pontiac Grand Prix JD Car, 1996, Ertl, Die, JD Dealerships & Employees Only, 5815AA, 1/18 Scale, NIB $175
□ ALSO SAME, Except Collectors Edition, Signed By Chad Little, 5816BA, 1/18 Scale, NIB $40
Notes:

□ JDX, 1975, Normatt, Plastic, Black, Battery-Powered, 7000-X Snowmobile, 1/10 Scale, Excellent-NIB $110-285
Notes:

□ 400, 1972, Normatt, Plastic, Green, Non-Powered Push Type, Or Battery-Powered Snowmobile, 7000, 1/10 Scale, Excellent-NIB $85-225
Notes:

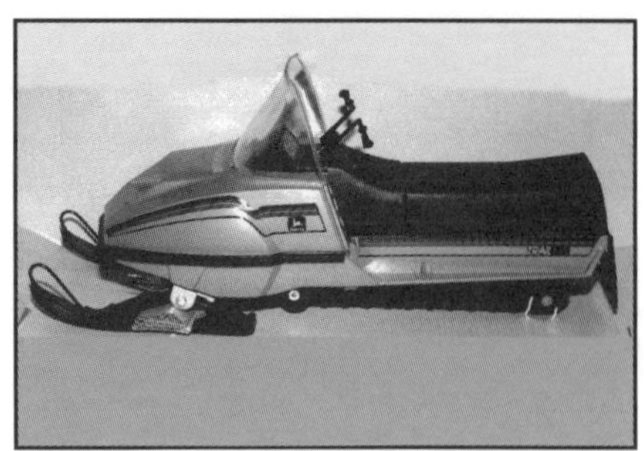

□ 440, 1981, Ertl, Plastic, Trailfire, Battery Powered Snowmobile,, Silver-Grey, 573, 1/10 Scale, Excellent-NIB $40-90
Notes:

□ 440, 1981, Suttle, Plastic, Cyclone, Metallic Green And Black, Push Or Battery Snowmobile, 8111, 1/10 Scale, Excellent-NIB $60-110
Notes:

□ John Deere Train, With Three Cars, And Two Tractors, JP655, NIB $65
Notes:

□ Airplane, 1992, SpecCast, Die, John Deere Logo, 35002, 12 Inch Wingspan, NIB $25
Notes:

□ JD Motorsports Golf Cart Bank, 1997, GMP, Die And Plastic, JD97, 1/16 scale, NIB $22
Notes:

□ Waterloo Works Fire Pumper, 2002, SpecCast, Die, Pump Handle Works, 1/12 Scale, JDM-134, NA
Notes:

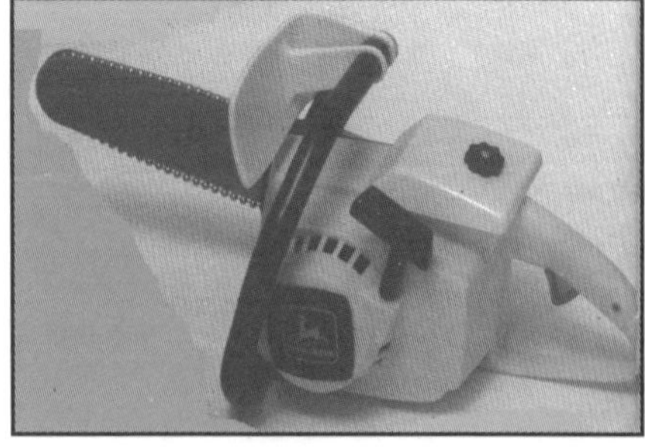

□ Chain Saw, 1974 Or 1979, Ertl, Die, Chain Saw, Sound, Working Chain, Some With John Deere Name On Cutting Bar, Some With Safety Guard, 526 Or 523, 15 3/4 Inches Long, Green NIB $45
□ ALSO SAME, Except Yellow, NIB $25
Notes:

□ Figurine, 1997, Ertl, Cold-Cast Porcelain, Uncle Earnest Figurine JD Tractor 1031, NA
Notes:

□ Figurine, 1997, Ertl, Cold-Cast Porcelain, Figurine 1046, NA
Notes:

□ Figurine, 1997, Ertl, Cold-Cast Porcelain, Figurine 1207, $15
Notes:

□ John Deere 4 X 4 Tractor Key Chain, 2002, Ertl, Die, Wheels Work, 15387, NIB $6
Notes:

□ 7800 Tractor Desk Pen Set, SpecCast, JDM-093, $30
Notes:

(Photo Courtesy Of SpecCast)

□ Gator Desk Pen Set, SpecCast, JDM-094, $30
Notes:

(Photo Courtesy Of SpecCast)

□ 890, 1975, Carter, Die, Tru-Scale, Green, NF, $100-220
Notes:

□ 891, 1975, Carter, Die, Tru-Scale, Green, NF, With Or Without 891 Decal, Excellent-NIB $100-265
Notes:

□ Bumble Toy, 1995, Ertl, 5701DO, $15
Notes:

More John Deere Tractors

For a variety of reasons--duplication, inability to find pix, poor photos, proliferation of custom-building of JD toys--some John Deere toys are not pictured in the main portion of the book. Most are listed here. Organized by Scale and Model of tractor.

1/16 Scale Tractors:

□ A, 1978, Lucht-Friesen, CI, NF, Plated Driver, Flywheel, Pulley, Steering Post, Steel Wheels, Custom, NA
□ A, 1978, Parker, SCA, Unstyled A, 179 Made, Custom, Excellent $140
□ A, 1980, ATT, SCA, Unstyled On Spoked Wheels And Rubber Tires, NIB $60
□ A, 1992, SC, C & M, Pete Freiheit Patterns Used, Custom, NIB $135
□ A, 1993, Ertl, Die, Canadian International Farm Equip Show (CIFES), 539PA, NIB $60
□ A, 2003, Ertl/RC, Die, With Man, Gold-Plated, 15569A, NA
□ A, 2003, Ertl/RC, Die, With Man, 15569, NA
□ A, 2004, Hamilton Authenticated, Die, With Umbrella, NA
□ A, 2004, Hamilton Authenticated, Resin, On Base, "Give Thanks For The Abundant Blessings That Fill Your Life, NA
□ AR, 1989, Dingman, Custom, Styled, Excellent $240
□ AR, 1992, Protractor, Spin, On Steel Or Rubber, NIB $225
□ AR, 1993, Ertl, Diesel, WF, 5680DO, NIB $30
□ B, 1950, Die, NF, Red, Pullmaster Tires, Denmark, Rare, NA
□ B, 1980s, ATT, SCA, Unstyled, Steel Wheels (2 Varieties), or Spoked With Rubber Tires, $35
□ B, 1992, C & M, Custom, Cumberland Valley Show. Tractor, NIB $110
□ B, 1992, C & M, Custom, Shelf Model, NIB $90
□ B, 1993, TCT, Custom, NF And WFE, Cast Wheels, NIB $50
□ B, 1998, Ertl, Die, Penn FFA Keystone 98, 29025, NIB $50
□ B, 2001, Franklin Mint, Tin, Windup, NIB $50
□ B, 2003, Ertl/RC, Die, Unstyled, "Precision Classic No. 24," NA
□ BW, 2004, Ertl/RC, Die, On Steel, Umbrella, 200th Anniversary, TBE15645A, NA
□ D, 1983, Jergenson, CA, WFE, Steel Wheels, Air Cleaner, Exhaust Stacks, Custom, NIB $20
□ D, 1983, Parker, WFE, Rubber Tires, Customized Ertl D, Excellent, $140
□ D, 1991, Sigomec, Die, WFE, Oval Decal Under, 1923/32, Excellent-NIB $50-65
□ D, 1987, SpecCast, Custom, Insert, "OTTPA," NIB $60
□ D, 1987, PC, SCA, Spoke Fly Wheel, Lake Region Dalton, MN, Excellent-NIB $35-45
□ D, 1993, Custom, Drayton, Canada Farm Show, NA
□ D, 1993, Rogers, Custom, WFE, Standard, Spoked Flywheel, NIB $45
□ D, 2002, Ertl/RC, Die, 1928 George White "2002 International Plowing Match/Rural Expo," NIB $65
□ 60, 2002, Ertl/RC, Die, Wide Front, 1/16, "Iowa FFA 2002"
□ G, 1999, Ertl, Die, Iowa FFA With Umbrella, Female Driver, NIB $65
□ G, 1989, NB & K, Custom, N/F, On Rubber, Tall Stacks, VA Show, 1200 Made, Excellent $180
□ GP, 1981, EJ, SCA, 1928 Model, NIB $40
□ GP, 2000, Ertl, Die, 1931, South Dakota FFA Foundation, 500 Made, NIB $60
□ GPWT, 1980, ATT, 2-Row, 1932-33 Model On Steel Wheels, NIB $45
□ H, 1993, TCT, Pewter, NF And WFE, NIB $15
□ H, 2000, Ertl, Die, With Umbrella, 2000 Iowa FFA Special Edition,10643A, NIB $55
□ H, 2000, Ertl, Die, High Crop, 2000 Expo X Show Tractor--Two Cylinder Club, NA
□ JD-Lanz, 1968, Tiny Car, D, WFE, Util., Brazl, Rare, NA
□ JD-Lanz, 1992, Deyzel, CA, WFE, Good Detail, South Africa, Detail, Custom, NA
□ JD-Lanz, 1963, Lesney, Die, Model 700, WFE, Utility, Gray Or Black Tires, 50, NIB $35
□ I, 2000, Ertl, Die, High Crop, 2000 Expo X Show Tractor--2 Cylinder Club, NIB $70
□ L, 1990, Mocast, SC, WFE, Excellent Detail, Worm Gear Steering, Custom, NA
□ L, 2004, SpecCast, Die, Hercules Engine, JDM 176, NA
□ LI, 2004, SpecCast, Die, JDM175, NA
□ LA, 2000, SpecCast, Die, 12th Ann Paxton-Buckley-Loda Show, Excellent-NIB $20-40
□ M, 1983, K & G, SCA, Steerable, Muffler And Fenders, Excellent-NIB $50-60
□ M, 1996, SpecCast, Die, 1996 Plow City Farm Toy Show & Auction, CUST396, NIB $50
□ MT, 1983, K & G, SCA, Steerable, Muffler And Fenders, NIB $45
□ MT, 1989, S Keith, Custom, Lafayette Show Tractor, 1100 Made, Excellent-NIB $80-100
□ MT, 1995, PDP, Custom, Geared Steering, NIB $150
□ MT, 1997, SpecCast, Die, Perry Country Old Iron Club, CUST415, NIB $40
□ MT, 1999, SpecCast, Die, Paxton-Buckley-Loda Show, 100 Made, NIB $40
□ 40, 1993, PDP, Custom, Row Crop, Excell-NIB $140-180
□ 40, 1985, K & G, SCA, 500 Made Excell-NIB $40-50
□ 40, 1989, AMTI, SCA, N/F Or WFE, Excellent-NIB $35-40
□ 40, 2002, Nolt, Hi-Crop, 250 Made, Custom, NIB $260
□ 145, Sigomec, Die, WFE, Utility, 3 Point, Firestone Tires, Argentina, NIB $85
□ 320, 1985, K & G, SCA, 500 Made, Excellent-NIB $40-50
□ 320, 1989, Trumm, Plastic, Plow City Sh, Exc-NIB $35-40
□ 420, 1994, PDP, Custom, 420-T, 750 Made, NIB $265
□ 420, 2002, Ertl/RC, Die, V Special, D, "Two-Cylinder Club Expo XIII —2003," NA
□ 420, 2004, Ertl/RC, Die, Row Crop, 1/16, No. 15481
□ 420V, 2003, Ertl/RC, Die, Hi-Crop, "2-Cylinder Club Expo XIII 2003," FB-2631, NA
□ 430, 1989, Engle, Custom, "Lebanon, PA, 1989" Show Tractor, Ltd To 1500, NIB $185
□ 430, 1989, AMTI, SCA, N/F or WFE, NIB $45
□ 435, 1958, Sigomec, Die, Similar To Ertl, No Decals, Rare, NIB $1200
□ 445, 1992, Sigomec, Die, WFE, Utility, Argentina, 445 Cast In, Model Also Later Recast, NA
□ 520, 1989, SC, FICL, WFE, 1st Collector Seal, NA
□ 520, 2002, Ertl/RC, Die, Wide Front, TBE15360, NA
□ 520, 2002, Ertl/RC, Hi-Clearance with Single Front Wheel "2002 Two-Cylinder Club," 16089, NA
□ 520, 2004, Ertl/RC, Die, Row Crop, TBE15599, NA
□ 530, 1987, Trumm, Plastic, WFE, Insert, Plow City 1987, 1965 Made, NIB $50
□ 620, Die, With Umbrella, "2002 PA State Farm Show," NIB $65
□ 620, 2003, Ertl/RC, Die, Wide Front & Umbrella, "Iowa FFA 2003," Limited to 1,500, NA
□ 620, 1998, Bloomstrand, Custom, Excellent $300
□ 630, 1994, EIG, Custom, Row Crop, LPG, "Lebanon Valley Farm Toy Show," NIB $225
□ 630 1997, Engle, Custom, Part Of The "30" Series, NIB $185
□ 720, 1999, Ertl, Die, "Wyoming FFA #5 1999," 29095HT, NIB $60
□ 720, 2002, Ertl/RC, Die, With 80 Blade and 45 Loader, "Precision Classics," 1/16, No. 98414, NA
□ 720, 2004, Hamilton Authenticated, Die, No. 45 Loader, No. 80 Rear Blade and Canvas Cab, NA
□ 730, 2002, Ertl/RC, Die, "Precision Classics," No. 98403, NA
□ 830, 2004, Ertl/RC, Die, Rice, Special Tractor, Two-Cylinder Expo XIV," NA
□ 830, 2004, Ertl/RC, Die, 1/16, 200th Birthday, TBE15577A, NA
□ 2010, 2002, Nolt, RC, Custom, NA
□ 2020, 1967, Wader, Plastic, WFE, Utility, Denmark, Rare, NA
□ 2030, 1973, Sigomec, Die, Made In Argentina, NIB $100
□ 2420, 1991, Sigomec, Die, NIB $120

□ 2520, 2003, ScaMo, Die, Diesel With ROPS, "20th Annual Back-East Show", NA
□ 3010, 1970, Sigomec, Die, WFE, No Fenders, Argentina, Also Recast, With Fenders, NIB $300
□ 3010, 1997, ScaMo, Die, Ag Safety Center, ROPS, Row Crop, FY-1002, NIB $60
□ 3010, 1994, Ertl, Custom, 7th Formosa Show, Ontario, NIB $75
□ 3010, 2002, Ertl/RC, Die, "Precision Classics," No. 98450, NA
□ 3020, 1992, C&M, Custom, WFE and Cab, Excellent-NIB $210-240
□ 3020, 1988, ScaMo, Die, "3rd Summer Toy Festival," NIB $30
□ ALSO SAME, Except "1988 World Ag Expo," NA
□ ALSO SAME, Except 1989, Steel Wheels, "Lancaster Show" Tractor, Excellent-NIB $20-30
□ 3020, 1994, Ertl, Die, Colfax FFA Alumni Toy Show, Excellent-NIB $40-50
□ 3020, 1969, Sigomec, Die, Argentina, Air Breather, Excellent $450
□ 3130, 1993, Sandcast, South Africa, NA
□ 3020, 1992, C& M, Custom, WFE And Cab, Excellent-NIB $180-210
□ 4010, 1984, Parker, CA, WFE, Kit, NIB $150
□ 4010, Danbury Mint, Clock In Rear Wheels, NIB $55
□ 4010, 2003, Ertl/RC, Die, High Crop, "National Farm Toy Museum," 4th In High Crop Series, 16109A, NA
□ 4010, 2004, Ertl/RC, Die, Diesel High Crop Tractor, TBE15602, NA
□ 4020, 1980s, ScaMo, Green, NA
□ ALSO SAME, Except "1988 World Ag Expo," NA
□ 4020, 1994, Ertl, Die, 3020 Gas, "Colfax FFA Alumni Farm Toy Show," NIB $50
□ 4020, 2004, Ertl/RC, Die, Row Crop, ROPS, Canopy, No. 15480, NA
□ 4020, 2004, Ertl/RC, Die, Cab, 200th Birthday, TBE15647A, NA
□ 4040, 2001, Die, FWD, "*Toy Tractor Times* Anniversary 2001," No. 29174P, NIB $60
□ 4430, 1972, Ertl, Die, NF, Only 19 Made, NIB $300
□ 4430, 1978, Ertl, Die, WFE, Cab, Small Lettering on Side Decals, 521, NA
□ 4430, 1990, Ertl, Die, Elmira Toy Celebration, FWA, Private, NIB $120
□ 4440, 1989, EFS, Custom, WFE, Large Flotation Front Wheels, Dual Rear, 1989 Elmira Toy Celebration, 275 Made, NIB $120
□ 4440, 2002, Ertl/RC, Die, "Precision Classics," No. 98406, NA
□ 4620, 2003, Ertl/RC, Die, Cab, "Iowa State Blue Ribbon Foundation," NA
□ 4620, 2003, Ertl/RC, Die, Cab And Deep Dish Wheels, "Ltd. Edition-IA State Fair," Serial Numbered I thru 3,500, NA
□ 4850, 1988, EFS, Custom, WFE, FWA, Duals, 1988 Elmira Toy Celebration, NIB $125
□ 5010, 1990, Benninger, Die, Customized Ertl 5020, 3rd Formosa, Ontario Toy Show, 125 Made, NA
□ 5020, 1992, Benninger, Die, Customized Ertl 5020, 5th Formosa (Ontario) Toy Show, 175 Made, NA
□ 5020, 1990, Ertl, Die, WFE, Standard, New Frame Design (Bolt Heads Not Recessed), With Or Without Dash Levers, 555, NIB $170
□ 6030, 1992, Stephan, Custom, C & K Farm Classics 20th Anniversary, 750 Made, NIB $480
□ 6030, 1993, C & M, Custom, Duals, With Or Without Cab, Various Options, NIB $400
□ 6030, 2004, Stephan, Die, Cab, Duals, 1/16, Limited To 500, Custom
□ 6030, 2004, Ertl/RC, Die, "24th Annual Plow City Show," NA
□ 7800, 1992, EFS, Custom, WFE, FWA, Elmira Toy Celebration Only Decal, 235 Made, NA
□ 7920, 2004, Ertl/RC, Die, MFD, Duals, Collector Edition, No. 15470A, NA
□ 8010, 1983, Sharp, Sheet Metal, WFE, 4WD, Articulated, Custom, NIB $450
□ 8420, 2002, Ertl/RC, Die, TBE15207, NA
□ 8890 4WD Friction Drive, 551, NIB $24
□ 9400, 1997, Ertl, Die, 4WD, With 3 Point Hitch, Collector Series, 5914BA, Excellent-NIB $110-165
□ Dain, 1996, ScaMo, Die, Nashville 96, DSO615, NIB65, NIB $65

1/15 Scale Tractors

□ 6920, 2002, Bruder, Plastic, 1/15, 02050, NA
□ 6920, 2002, Bruder, Plastic, 1/15, With Loader, 02051, NA
□ 6920, 2002, Bruder, Plastic, 1/15, With Loader And Duals, 02053, NA
□ 6920, 2002, Bruder, Plastic, 1/15, Duals, 02054, NA
□ 6920, 2002, Bruder, Plastic, 1/15, With Tipping Trailer, 02058, NA
□ 6920, 2002, Bruder, Plastic, 1/15, With Dump Wagon, 02098, NA

1/32 Scale Tractors:

□ A, 1986, ScaMo, Die, NF, Steel Wheels, Or Styled A On Rubber, Excellent-NIB $6-10
□ A, 1994, Stephan, Die, Custom, 1000 Made, NIB $65
□ 3150, 1989, Ertl, Die, FWA, Cab, 3 Point. Excellent-NIB $7-10
□ 3200, 1994, Siku, Die, Limited Production, NIB $50
□ 3350, 1991, Ertl, Die, W/Loader, Three Attachments, Limited To Dealers Only, NIB $20
□ 4320, European Tour 1993, Limited Edition, 5725MA, NIB $85
□ 4430, 1985, Sigomec, Die, Argentina, WFE, 400, NIB $35
□ 4440, 1979, Ertl, Die, No Cab, NF, Scarce, No 66, NIB $40
□ 5720, 2004, Siku, Die, 4452, Siku Farmer Plus Series
□ 5820, 2004, Siku, Die, 3050
□ 6200, 1995, Ertl, Die, European Version, 5688, NIB $20
□ 6210, 1999, Ertl Elite, Die, With loader, 00076, NIB $15
□ 6920S, 2002, Siku, Die, W/ Front Hitch, 3252, NIB $20
□ 6520, 2004, Tim Toys, Die, Front Hitch, 35011, NA
□ 6620, 2004, Siku, Die, Industrial, "Siku Museum," In 3252 Box, NA
□ 6820, 2004, Siku, Die, Duals Front & Rear, "2003 Agritechnica Sondermodel," NA
□ 6820, 2004, Siku, Die, Duals, 'L.C.N. Zwolle 2003," Custom, NA
□ 6820, 2004, Siku, Die, Duals, Front Weight, , NA
□ 6920, 2004, Siku, Die, Front Weight, "JO. Manheim Special," NA
□ 6920, 2004, Siku, Die, 4455, Siku Farmer Plus Series, NA
□ 6920S, 2003, Siku, Die, Front Weights, 3252, NA
□ 6920S, 2004, Siku, Die, Loader, 3652, NA
□ 6620S, 2003, Siku, Die, Front And Rear Duals, , NA
□ 7040, 2003, Ertl/RC, Die, 4-Wheel-Drive, "2003 National Farm Toy Show," , NA
□ 7520, 2004, Die, Collector Edition, NA
□ 7920, 2004, Britains/RC, Die, European Tractor, 15525, NA
□ 9400, Flying Toys, Netherlands, NIB $50

1/43 Scale Tractors:

□ C, 1993, SpecCast, Pewter, JDM022, NIB $20
□ H, 1994, SpecCast, Pewter, Single Front Wheel, JDM053, NIB $15
□ H, 1994, SpecCast, Pewter, Single Front Wheel, JDM053, NIB $15
□ M, 1994, SpecCast, Die, JDM031, NIB $15
□ MT, 1995, SpecCast, Pewter, JDM062, NIB $17

- Waterloo Boy, 1981, Don Winter, Metal, WFE, Steel Wheels, NA
- 2010, 1995, SpecCast, Pewter, JDM067, NIB $20
- 2120, 1973, Nacoral, Plastic, WFE, Utility, Green With Silver Plating, Spain, Rare, 2120, NA
- 3185, 1984, NPS, Die, WFE, FWA, Green, Cab, Hong Kong, Marketed Under Other Names Also, 3009, NA
- 4055, 1995, SpecCast, Pewter, Regular Edition, JDMO68, NIB $20
- 4230, 1998, Ertl, Die, 21st National Show Tractor, 5507AA, NIB $23
- 4320, 1998, Ertl, Die, "European Tour" On Left Fender, In Silver Box, 5725MA, 500 Made, NIB $35
- 6400, 1994, Ertl, Die, FWA, Cab, Steerable, 5668EO, NIB $12
- 7800, 1994, SpecCast, Pewter, Plain Top Tractor, JDM048, NIB $16
- 7800, 1994, SpecCast, Die, JDM033, NIB $30
- 8010, 1994, SpecCast, Die, JDM030, NIB $65
- 8010, 1994, SpecCast, Die, Plow City 7/94, NIB $75
- 8020, 1995, SpecCast, Pewter, With Duals, Painted Pewter, NIB $65
- 8400, 1998, SpecCast, Pewter, JDM115, NIB $35
- ALSO SAME, Except On Base, JDM111, NIB $22
- ALSO SAME, Except Stocking Holder, JDM111, NIB $22
- 8520, 2003, SpecCast, Pewter, Front & Rear Duals, JDM 185, NA

1/50 Scale Tractors:

- B, 2004, Athearn, Die, No. 7750, NA

1/64 Scale Tractors:

- A, 1983, Midwest Importers, Die, NF, Thailand Copy of Ertl, NIP $4
- A, 1993, C&M, Spincast, NIP $20
- AR, 1988, Buhler, SC, Custom, Unstyled, WFE, Rubber or Steel Wheels, NIP $25
- D, 1991, Sigomec, Die, WFE Standard, 1923/64, NIP $15
- GP, 1988, ScaMo, NF, Wide Tread, On Steel Or Rubber, NIP $12
- LA, 1980, Custom-Cast, Green And Yellow, NIP $40
- MT, 1989, Keith SC, NF or WFE, 1989 Lafayette Show, Custom, NIP $30
- R, Anniversary, Fancy Card, 2nd/Series, Error, 1514A, NIP $20
- 40, 1993, PD, Custom, With Loader, NA
- 60, 1967, Ertl, Die, Row Crop, Riveted Or Spun-On Rears, Hitch Hook, 1305, NIP $60
- ALSO SAME, Except Riveted Or Stamped Rear Axles, W/O Hitch Hook, 1305, NIP $60
- ALSO SAME, Except Some With Series 30 Fenders, 1305, NIP $50
- ALSO SAME, Except 1988, RB, Pewter, Copy of Ertl, NA
- 60 Series, 1990, Ertl, Die, WFE, Cab, New Paint Pattern, Decal Revision, 5623DO, NA
- ALSO SAME, Except "JD Parts Expo, Phoenix, AZ, Strobe Bars On Decal, 5612MA, NIP $20
- 80, 1986, Ertl, Die, "National Farm Toy Museum," 1213MA, NIP $8
- 320, 1989, Keith, SC, WFE, Utility, Custom, NIP $30
- 330, 1989, Keith, SC, WFE, Utility, Custom, NIP $30
- 430, 1988, Keith, SC, NF, 1988 New Ulm Show, Custom, NIP $30
- 430, 1998, Ertl, *Replica* Subscriber Issue, NIP $20
- 530, 1997, Ertl, Die, WF, Duals, Shelf Model, 5194, NIP $6
- 530, NF, In Fancy Box,1997 Iowa FFA Ed, 5186GA, NIP $15
- ALSO SAME, Except 1998, "Iowa FFA Foundation," 5186GA, NIP $15
- 620, 1988, Buhler, SC, WFE Standard, Cstm, NIP $30
- 630, 1985, Baker, WFE, Represents 1959-60 Model, DJB Stamped On Bottom, NIP $30
- 630, 1988, Buhler, SC, WFE Standard, Custom, NIP $30
- 700 Series, 1980, Keith/Matsen, Series A, Industrial Yellow, NIP $30
- 730, 1988, Baker, SC, NF or WFE, Custom, NIP $30
- 2510, 1989, Keith/Matsen, SC, WFE, Custom, NIP $30
- 3010, 1988, Buhler, SC WFE, Standard, Custom, NIP $30
- 3010, 1989, Keith/Matsen, SC, LPG, NF, Custom, NIP $30
- 4010, 1988, Keith, NF, Custom, NIP $30
- 4010, 1988, Keith, NF, Custom, Larger Tires, "Apache Mall 1988 Show," NIP $30
- 4020, 1990, C & M, Custom,, Diesel, WFE, or Row Crop, NIP $30
- 4230, Diesel, W/Cab, '98 European Edition, 5131YA, NIP $32
- 4255, 1990, Ertl, Die, WFE, Cab Black With Green Top, 1619. (4255 On Bubble Pack Card), NIP $6
- 4430, 1973, Ertl, Die, Sound Idea Tractor, WFE, ROPS Frame, Kit, 8005, NA
- 4430, 1988, RB, Pewter, WFE, Cab, Copy of Ertl, NA
- 4430, Sigomec, Bubble-Wrapped Box, NIP $30
- 4450, 1987, Ertl, Die, WFE, Cab, Farm Festival '87 Bubble Pack, NIP $10
- 4450, 1987, Ertl, Die, WFE, Cab, Young Farmer Bubble Pack Europe, 4106A1, NIP $8
- 4450, 1989, Ertl, D, Pow-R-Pull, Young Farmer Bubble Pack For European Market, 4090, NIP $10
- 4450, 1991, Ertl, Die, Tractor With Sound, Runs On Battery, 5693EO, NIP $8
- 4450, 1991, Ertl, Die, WFE, Cab, Front-Mounted Loader, Faceted Light Bar On Front, 587, NIP $8
- ALSO SAME, Except 1992, "Royal" On Hood, "1992 Royal Agricultural Expo, Toronto," NIP $30
- 4455, 1991, Ertl, Die, WFE, Cab, FWA, Faceted Light Bar On Front, 5517, NIP $6
- ALSO SAME, Except Duals, 5516, NIP $9
- 4455, Front Weights, Row Crop, Solid Rear Rims, 5571, NIP $5
- ALSO SAME, Except Slotted Rear Rim, NIP $7
- 4455, Front Weights, With FWA, Solid Rear Rim, 5612, NIP $8
- ALSO SAME, Except Duals, 5606, NIP $11
- ALSO SAME, Except, Front Weights, With Loader, 5613, NIP $9
- 5020, 2000, Ertl, Die, *Replica* Issue Number 100, 2,400 Made, NIP $20
- ALSO SAME, Except Gold, 100 Made, NIP $450
- 5020, 1989, Keith, SC, WFE, With Cab, Or Duals, Or Rops, Custom, NIP $30
- 6030, 1986, Gunning, SC, WFE, Cab, Duals, W/ W/O 3 Point, NIP $30
- 6030, 1989, Keith, SC, WFE, W/ Or W/O Cab, Custom, NIP $30
- 6030, 1989, Keith, SC, WFE, Duals, ROPS, NIP $30
- 6030, 1989, Keith, SC, WFE, Cab, "4th Annual McMean County Show," Custom, NIP $30
- 7020, 1984, Baker, SCA, 4WD, No Cab, Decal Variations, NIP $65
- 7020, 1989, Baker, SCA, 4WD, Butcher Toys 8-8-"1989 8th Annual Show, Breckinridge, MI," NIP $100
- 7020, 2003, Ertl/RC, Die, 4-Wheel-Drive, "2003 National Farm Toy Show," NA
- 7210, 1999, Ertl, Die, "1998 John Deere Reno," NIP $30
- 7520, 1980, Baker, SCA, Kit, Custom, With or Without Cab, NIP $65
- 7520, 1980, Walters, SC, WFE, 4WD, Articulated, Cab, Crude, Excellent $65
- 7520, 1989, Baker, SCA, 4WD, Butcher Toys 8-8-1989 8th Annual Show, Breckinridge, MI, NIP $100
- 8010, 1988, Keith, SC, 4WD, Articulated, Custom, NIP $150
- 8010, 4WD, 1994 Plow City Show, SC, NIP $150
- 8630, Darrell J Baker, Kit, NIP $45
- Froelich, 1967, Ertl, Die, With Or Without Steering Wheel Knob, Ribbed Or Smooth Wheels, 1301, NIP $50
- Froelich, 1988, RB, Pewter, WFE, Antique Tractor, Copy Of Ertl, NIP $15
- Froelich, 1992, Sigomec, Die, WFE, Antique Style, Argentina, 1892, NA
- Waterloo Boy, 1990, Spec, Pwt, CEZDM007 NIP $20
- Waterloo Boy, 1992, Sigomec, Die, WFE, Antique

Style, Argentina, 1914, NIP $20

1/87 Scale Tractors:

 A, 1981, Woodlands, Metal, NF, Steel Wheels, Kit, D-208, Rubber Wheels D-211, NIP $30
 B, 2004, Athearn, Die, 7700, NA
 50, 2004, Athearn, Die, 7701, NA
 6420, 2004, Athearn, Die, 7703, NA
 6920S, 2004, Wiking, Plastic, 393-01-32, NA
 6920S, 2004, Siku, Die, 1870, NA
 Waterloo Boy, 2004, Athearn, Die, 7702, NA

1/160 Scale Tractor:

 6920S, 2004, Wiking, Plastic, 1/160, 9580125, NA

1/8 Scale Tractor:

 D, 2000, Stoller, Die, Custom With Working Features, 20 Made, NA
 D, 2002, ScaMo, Die, Industrial, FY-1024, NA
 70. 2004, ScaMo, Die, "Farm Progress Show 2003," FY-1026, NA

1/10 Scale Tractors:

 AW, 1982, Kruse, Wood, NF, Rubber Wheels, Custom, NA
 GM, 1982, Kruse, Wood, NF, On Rubber, Custom, NA

1/12 Scale Tractors:

 A, 1980, OTC, CA, NF, On Steel Or Rubber, Custom, Robert Gray Molds, Mankato Show, 100 Made, NA
 A, 1986, PC, CA, NF, On Rubber Or Steel, Custom, Robert Gray Molds, Excellent $35
 A, Taiwan, Variously Show "GP," "OP" "CP" In Raised Letters, $10

Pedal Tractors:

 Accessory Pack, 2002, Ertl/RC, Die, Pedal Tractor, (Duals), TBE15454, NA
 ROPS, 1991, Ertl, Die, ROPS Kit For Dealers, Goes W/4020 WF Pedal, NIP $225
 Tractor, 2002, Ertl/RC, Plastic, Pedal, And Wagon, TBEK34829, NA
 Tractor, 2002, Ertl/RC, Plastic, Pedal, With Loader, TBEK34828, NA
 Tractor, 2003, Peg-Perego, Plastic, Power-Pull, 12-Volt, Ride-On, 2-Speed, NA
 Tractor, 2004, Ertl/RC, Plastic, Pedal, Toys For Tots, 1/4, NA
 Trailer, 1950, Eska, PS, Trailer, 2 Wheel, W/Flare Sided Fenders For Above, NIB $250
 Trailer, 1960, Eska, PS, Trailer, 2 Wheel, W/Straight Sided Fender, Excellent-NIB $200-425
 Umbrella, Eska, Cloth, Umbrella For Pedal Tractor, Excellent-NIB 220-325
 Wagon, 2004, Ertl/RC, Die, Riding, TBE535, NA
 730, 1958, Eska, SCA, 38," NF, 5 Variations, Excellent-NIB $450-700
 730, Eska, SCA, 38," NF, Small Hole Variation, NA
 4300, 2004, Ertl/RC, Plastic, Pedal, 1/4, NA
5020, 2004, Ertl/RC, Die, Vintage Riding Tractor, TBE15502, NA
 8520, 2002, Ertl/RC, Die, Pedal Tractor With MFWD And New Tires, TBE15392, NA

Implements& Machinery:

Organized by scale, then name of machine, then year of first toy manufacture.

1/16 Scale Impl. & Machinery:

 Baler, 2002, Ertl/RC, Die, Model 348, Updated Graphics, TBE15518, NA
 Baler, 2004, Ertl/RC, Die, Round, New Graphics, TBE15689, NA
 Chopper, 1993, PD, Custom, #15, Lic by GSR/Jeff Krebbs, Penn-Dutch, NIB $75
 Combine, 1975, Jergensen, SC, Pull-Type, Custom, NA
 Combine, 1985, Hooker/Cottonwood Acres, SCA, Model 55, With Zinc Parts, Both Heads, NIB $425
 Combine, 1988, Coble, SCA, 42 Pull Type, Excellent $225
 Combine, 1988, Baird, Sandcast, Model 42, Pull-Type, 300 Made, Rare, Excellent $225
 Combine, 1988, Cleek, Self-Propelled, Custom, NA
 Combine, 1993, Sigomec, (Argentina) Die, Self-Propelled Combine, 1065, NA
 Corn Picker, 1998, Bloomstrand, Custom, 227, Exc $300
 Corn Picker, 1952, Carter, PS, Model 227, Pull Type, Two Row, Prototype, Rare, Excellent $1200
 Corn Sheller, 1998, Bloomstrand, Custom, Mounted, NIB $400
 Cotton Picker, 1989, Vintage Company, Sheet Metal, Self-Propelled, Basket Dumps, Custom, NA
 Cotton Picker, 1989, Lemmond, PS, Model 9920, Limited Edition, NIB $500
 Crane, 2002, Nolt, 1-A Rear Mounted 3-Point Hitch Crane, Custom, NA
 Disc, 1992, Rouch, Custom, KBA, 7' Wheel Pull, Exc $300
 Disc, 1992, Nolt, Custom, KBL, Harrow, 3 Point, NIB $100
 Disc, 1995, Viking, Custom, BWA, NA
 Disc, 1968, Ertl, Die, RWA, Wings Fold Up Both Sides, C-Hitch, Various Decals, 556, Excellent-NIB $100-165
 Drill, 2002, Ertl/RC, Die, Grain, TBE15350, NA
 Elevator, 2003, Ertl/RC, Die, Hay, TBE15552, NA
 Engine, 1986, Riecke, Custom, One Cylinder, No Trucks, Or On Trucks, Or Battery Powered, Excell. $55
 Forage Harvester, 1993, PDP, Custom, No 15 Hay Chopper, Excellent $120
 Grain Auger, 1987, Nygren, SC, Custom, NA
 Grain Binder, 1980, Lowry, Metal, Green, PTO, Custom, Excellent $110
 Grain Drill, 1992, Rouch, Custom, Van Brundt EE, NA
 Grain Drill, 1995, Viking, Pony Press, 36541, NA
 Grinder-Mixer, 1982, Standi, PS, Action Augers, NA
 Hammermill, 1983, Graves, SCA, 10A, Excellent $75
 Hammermill, 1984, OTC, Vintage Style With Transport Wheels, Custom, NA
 Harrow, 1991, Haag,Custom, Spring Tooth, Three Section, NA
 Hay Loader, 1986, Hoover, NA
 Hay Mower, 1980, Nygren, No. 5, Green, Excellent $150
 Hay Mower, 1980, Nygren, No. 7, Green, Excellent $150
 Hay Mower, 1995, PDP, Custom, No 5, Lever Lift Or Cylinder Lift, Green Or Yellow Excellent-NIB, $90-110
 Hay Rake, 1990, Rouch, Custom, Highly Detailed, Working parts, Custom, NA
 Loader, 1950, Eisele, PS Or SCA, Fits A, Crank & String, Variations, Excellent-NIB $200-$350
 Loader, 1993, PDP, Custom, Excellent-NIB $100-120

 Plow, 1994, Viking, Custom, 650 AH, 3, 4, Or 5 Bottom, Custom, NA
 Plow, 1995, Vikingland, Custom, 810, Excellent $175
 Plow, 1997, Vikingland, Custom, 100, 16' Chisel, Excellent $200
 Plow, 1987, Deere & Co., Walking Plow, Mounted On Walnut Base, "John Deere 150th Anniversary," 12 Inches Long, NIB $65
 Plow, 1930s, Deere, CI, 10," Walking, Nickel Plated, Gift To JD Supervisors, NIB $200
 ALSO SAME, Except Aluminum With Chrome Plating, NIB $175
 Plow, 1930, Deere & Co., CI, Walking, Presented To Future Farmers Of America Chapters, 10 Inches Long, NIB $240
 ALSO SAME, Except Presented To New (Negro) Farmers Of America Chapters, NIB $240
 Plow, 1960, Deere & Co., Die, Walking, Presented To FFA Chapters, 12 Inches Long, NIB $240
 Plow, 1970, Deere, Chrome-Plated, Walking Plow, Local Chapter Of FFA, NA
 Plow, 1978, McClendon, Die, Walking, Similar To Above, 100 Made, "MAX" Case On Bottom Of Attached Base Plaque, 12 Inches Long, NA
 Plow, 1955, Carter, PS, 2 Bottom, Lever And Cylinder, 2 Tire Variations, Excellent-NIB $195-$320
 Plow, 1992, Nolt, Custom, 3 Bottom, 3 Point, Model 416, NA
 Plow, 2000, ScaMo, Die, Gilpen, FY-0036, NA
 Plow, 2000, Spec-Cast, Horse-Drawn, 20th Annual Plow City Show, NA
 Running Gear, 1992, Rouch, Custom, Model 963, Custom, NA
 Thresher, 1999, Pauley, Custom, NIB $375
 Trailer, 1987, ScaMo, Plastic, Two Wheel Bottom Dump Trailer, Green/With Yellow Wheels Or Yellow With Yellow Wheels, 351, NA
 Wagon, 1950, SC, Barge, Spring-Mounted Box, Removable Low Sides, Solid Rubber Tires, Clevis-Style Hitch or Pin-Style Hitch, Rare, NA
 Wagon, 1952, Carter, PS, Flare Box, Rubber Wheels, 2 Wheel Variations, Excellent-NIB $90-$165
 Wagon, 1953, Carter, SS, Removable Aluminum Box, One Piece Tongue, Very Scarce, Excellent-NIB $100-$200
 Wagon, 1955, Carter, PS, Flare Box, Tin Wheels,Tire And Box Variations, Excellent-NIB $90-$165
 Wagon, 1964, Ertl, Die, 112, Forage, Metal Wheels, Boy Box, 533, Excellent-NIB $150-$300
 Wagon, 1974, Ertl, Die, Barge, Die Cast, Varieties, Came with Utility, NIB $25
 Wagon, 1978, Gray, Grain Box, On Steel, Driver, Mules, Horses, SCA, NIB $140
 Wagon, 1984, Ertl, PS, Forage, 533, NA
 Wagon, 1990, ScaMo, Die, Buckboard, DSO250, NIB $25
 ALSO SAME, Except Gold Plated, NIB $75
 Wagon, 1991, ScaMo, Die, Surrey, Reliance, "Phoenix 90" Cast In, DSO416, NIB $25
 Wagon, 1991, ScaMo, Die, Surrey, DSO416, Excellent-NIB $12-$20
 Wagon, 1997, Ertl, Die, Corn Load, Foxfire Driver, TBE5341, NA
 Wagon, 2000, ScaMo, Die, Corn Wagon With Horses, FY-0044, NA
 Wagon, 2000, ScaMo, Die, Surrey With Horse, FY-0030, NA
 Wagon, 2000, ScaMo, Die, Mail Wagon With Horse, FY-0041, NIB $30
 Wagon, 2003, Ertl/RC, Die, Hay, TBE15485, NA
 Wagon, 2002, Ertl/RC, Plastic, For Pedal Tractor, TBEK34830, NA

1/25 Scale Impl. & Machinery:

 Cotton Picker, 9976 Pro-Ser, 6-Row, Memphis '97, Box, 5765EA, NIB $40

1/32 Scale Impl. & Machinery:

 Baler, 2003, Britains/RC, Die, 348 Square, 05369, NA
 Combine, 2002, Ertl/RC, Die, 9750 STS, "Series II Precision," No. 98405, NA
 Combine, 2004, Ertl/RC, Die, 9860 STS, Collector Edition, No. 15520A, NA
 Combine, 2004, Britains/RC, Die, 9880 STS, 40845, NA
 Elevator, 1990, Ertl, Die, With Bales, 5608DO, NIB $20
 Spreader, 1990, Ertl, Die, Manure, Side Discharge, 5625, Excellent-NIB $5-$10
 Trailer, 1996, Die, Trailer, Dump Trailer Introduction Model, 1000 Made, Excellent-NIB $5-$20
 Wagon, 1994, Ertl, Plastic, With Bales, 5694, Excellent-NIB $5-8
 Wagon, 1985, Sigomec, Barge, Industrial Yellow, Rear Hitch, Decal Rear Endgate, 512, NIB $20
 Wagon, 2003, Siku, Die, 7600 Forage Harvester, 4056, NA
 Wagon, 2002, Ertl/RC, Die, 963 Barge, "Precision Classics," No. 97965, NA
 Wagon, 2004, Siku, Die, 7400 Forage Harvester With Grass Pickup, 4057, NA
 Wagon, 2004, Siku, Die, 7500 Forage Harvester, NA

1/43 Scale Impl. & Machinery:

 Thresher, 1992, Spec-Cast, Pewter, Fine Pewter, With Show Logo, JDM-016, NIB $60
 ALSO SAME, Except No Logo, NIB $85
 ALSO SAME, Except With Brass Plate, JDM 017, NIB $50
 Wagon, 1992, Ertl, Die, Vintage Flare Box Wagon, 5637EO, $3-6

1/50 Scale Impl. & Machinery:

 Dumper, 2002, SpecCast, Pewter, JDM140, 1/50 Scale, NA
 Plow, 2002, SpecCast, Pewter, 1/50 Scale, JDM158, NA

1/64 Scale Impl. & Machinery:

 Auger, 1984, Standi, Plastic, NIP $9
 Baler, 1983, Ertl, Die, Round, No Model Numbers, 1212, NIP $9
 Baler, 1988, Ertl, Die, Round Baler With Hook-Type Hitch, Get-A-Round Promotion, NIP $30
 Combine, 1982, Ertl, Die, 2 Heads, Yellow Cab Top, 537, NIP $33
 Combine, 1997, Ertl, Die, 9600, Two Heads, TBES809, NIP $25
 Combine, 1998, Ertl, Die, CTS II, Rice, 5172 NIP $18
 Combine, 1987, Nygren, SC, Model 12A Pull-Type, Custom, NIP $30
 Corn Picker/Sheller, 1986, Nygren, SC, 2-Row Model 227, Mounts On Ertl 1/64 JD 3020, Custom, NIP $20
 Corn Planter, 1986, Matsen, Pewter, Model 7000, 6, 12 Or 24 Row, Folding, Custom, NA
 Corn Sheller, 1986, Nygren, SC, Model 71, Custom, NIP $20

 Cotton Picker, 2002, Ertl/RC, Die, Model 9986, TBE15440, NA
 Cultivator, 1992, Standi, Plastic, Four Row Crop Cultivator, Three-Point Hitch, NIP $6
 Cultivator, 1992, Standi, Plastic, Six Row Crop Cultivator, Three-Point Hitch, NIP $6
 Cultivator, 1992, Standi, Plastic, Eight Row Crop Cultivator, Three-Point Hitch, NIP $6

☐ Disc, 1988, Standi, Plastic, Narrow Or Wide Transport With Transport Wheels, NIP $6
☐ Elevator, 1988, Standi, Plastic, Exc $10
☐ Engine, 1994, Spec, Die, EP Gasoline, New Orleans 1994, Scale Unknown, Perhaps 1/64 Scale, NA
☐ ALSO SAME, Except 1995, EP, Gasoline, NIP $15
☐ Flail Chopper, 1985 And 1988, Nygren, SC Or CA, Model 15, Custom, NIP $20
☐ Flail Mower, 1988, Standi, Plastic, NIP $6
☐ Forage Blower, 1988, Standi, Plastic, NIP $6
☐ Grain Drill, 1989, Standi, Plastic, Green With Yellow Wheels, NIP $6
☐ Grain Drill, 1986, Nygren, SC, Green Top, Custom, NIP $20
☐ Mower, 1985, Nygren, SC, Mid-Mount, Custom, NIP $20
☐ Mower, 1988, Nygren, SC, Gyro, Rotary, Custom, NIP $20
☐ Mulch Ripper, 2003, Ertl/RC, Die, 2700, TBE15491, NA
☐ Spreader, MT, Plastic, Manure, Generic, 7300, NIP $11
☐ Stalk Chopper, 1988, Standi, Plastic, NIP $6
☐ Stalk Chopper, 1988, Nygren, SC, Custom, NIP $6
☐ Stacker, 1988, Standi, Plastic, Hay Stacker, Green And Yellow, NIP $7
☐ Stack Mover, 1988, Standi, Plastic, Tool Bar, 1989, NIP $6
☐ Tool Bar, 1989, Gunning/Clifton, Anhydrous With 11 Or 15 Shanks, NIP $50
☐ Trailer, 1963, Lesney, Die, Two Wheel Trailer, Gray Wheels Or Black Tires, With JD Lanz 500, Stock No. 51, NIP $15
☐ Trailer, 1992, Ertl, Die, Machine Trailer, Tandem Axle With Adjustable Rear Ramp, Black, 4161FO, NIP $5
☐ Wagon, 1980, Sigomec, Flare Model 529, Yellow Flare Wagon, Plastic Wheels, Rubber Tires, 2520, NIP $10
☐ ALSO SAME, Except Green Flare Wagon, 2929, NIP $10
☐ Wagon, 1987, Sigomec, Barge Wagon, Green, Rear Hitch, 2950, NIP $10
☐ ALSO SAME, Except Yellow, 2951, NIP $10
☐ Wagon, 1984, Nygren, SC, Flare, Custom, NIP $20
☐ Wagon, 1986, Ertl, Plastic, Auger, Generic, 1136, NIP $20
☐ Wagon, 1988, Standi, Plastic, Bale Wagon, High Sides, NIP $8
☐ Wagon, 1988, Standi, Plastic, Forage, Tandem Rear Axles, Steerable, NIP $9
☐ Wagon, 1988, Standi, Plastic, Flare, With Hoist, NIP $8
☐ Wagon, 1994 Ertl, Die, Gravity, 5552, NIP $5
☐ Wagon, 2003, Ertl/RC, Die, Forage Harvester, 15494, NA

1/80 Scale Impl. & Machinery:

☐ Combine, 1982, Ertl, Die, 1 Head, Black Auger, 1519, NIP $85
☐ ALSO SAME Except Green Auger, NIP $34
☐ Combine, 1986, Ertl, Die, Self-Propelled Titan II, Interchangeable Corn Or Grain Head, Green Cab Roof, 550EO, NIP $25

1/87 Scale Impl. & Machinery:

☐ Corn Planter, 1981, Woodland, White Metal, Kit, Four-Row, Part of JD A tractor-corn planter set, D-207, NIP $30

HO Scale Impl. & Machinery:

☐ Combine, 1998, Ertl, Die, 9510, Powertech Engine, HO Scale, 5468CO, NA

Lawn & Garden Tractors

1/16 Lawn & Garden Tractors

☐ Trailer, 1965, Ertl, Die, Two Wheel Dump, Opening Endgate, Crank Or C-Type Hitch, Green, 542, NIB $35
☐ Trailer, 1971, Ertl, Die, Two Wheel Dump, Opening Endgate, Crank Or C-Type Hitch, White, 542, NIB $35 Lawn & Garden
☐ X485, 2002, Ertl/RC, Die, L & G Tractor With Attachments, TBE15353, NA
☐ X585, 2003, Ertl/RC, Die, L&G Tractor With Attachments, TBE15509, NA
☐ 55 Series, 1992, Ertl, Die, With Cart, NIB $35
☐ 3205, 1999, Ertl, Die, No Mower Deck, 13031A, Excellent-NIB $10-15
☐ 3235, 1999, Ertl, Die, With Mower Deck, Snow Blower, & Blade, 13015, NIB $10

1/32 Lawn & Garden Tractors

☐ Gator, 2001, Ertl/RC, Die, 6 x 4, "World Of Opportunity--JD Expo 2001--San Antonio," 15289A, NIB $20
☐ Gator, 2002, RC/Britains, Die, Gator and 455 Garden Tractor Assortment, 40521, NA

Industrials & Crawlers

Organized by scale, then model of crawler or tractor--MC or AR, for example, and name of implements--plow, wagon.

1/16 Scale Indus. & Crawlers:

☐ AR, 1992, Protractor, Spin, Industrial Tractor On Rubber, NIB $265
☐ AW, 1990, SC, Florida Classic, WFE, Unstyled, Collector Edition, Custom, Varieties, NIB $100
☐ Backhoe/Loader, 1997, GHQ, Pewter, 310A, Kit, 53-006, NIB $30
☐ Blade, 1954, Ertl, Die, Green Or Yellow, Fits 40 & 420, Early Decals Or Square Letter Decals, Excellent-NIB $100-175
☐ Blade, 1989, Hartz-Partz, Steel, 3-Point Hitch Back Blade, Swivels, Custom, NIB $40
☐ ALSO SAME, Except 1991, Yellow For Nolt Tractor, NIB $40
☐ Blade, 1991, Haag, Custom, For Scraper Model 45, Rear-Mounted 3-Point Scraper Blade, Adjustable, Custom, NIB $45
☐ Blade, 1994, PDP, Custom,#80, For Scraper, 3point Hitch, Green Or Yellow, Excellent-NIB $50-65
☐ Blade, SpecCast, Custom, For Scraper, Industrial, Fits 320 Or 420, Excellent-NIB $60-70
☐ Loader, 1992, Sigomec, Die, Industrial, 200, Re-Issue, NIB $100
☐ Loader, 1993, PD, Custom, Spincast, Model 40, NIB $80
☐ MC, 1983, K & G, SCA, Crawler, Serial Numbered, NIB $45
☐ MC, 1989, Riecke, Custom, Crawler, Highly Detailed, NIB $300
☐ MC, 1998, SpecCast, Die, Crawler, CE, "Lake Region," With Metal Tracks, JDM 164, NIB $38
☐ MC, 1998, SpecCast, Die, Crawler, FFA Millenium, NIB $50

☐ MC, 2001, SpecCast, Die, Crawler With Metal Tracks, JDM 164, NIB $38
☐ MCI, 1997, SpecCast, Die, Crawler, Lake Region Pioneer Thresher's Association, NIB $50
☐ MI, 1988, Riecke, SC, WFE, Utility, Orange Or Yellow, NA
☐ MI, 1990, Ertl, Die, Industrial Tractor, Orange With Fenders, 5628DO, Excellent-NIB $22-30
☐ Road Grader, 2004, Ertl/RC, Die, TBE15233, NA
☐ 40, 1954, Ertl, Die, 40, Crawler, Industrial Yellow, No Stock No, Excellent-NIB $350-750
☐ 40, 1983, Sandcast, K&G, Custom, NIB $35
☐ 40, 1990, Nolt, Custom, Crawler, Industrial, Yellow, 90 Made, By Stephan, Excellent-NIB $240-280
☐ 320, 1990, Nolt, Custom, Tractor, Industrial Yellow, By Stephan, Excellent-NIB $200-265
☐ 430, 1983, Nygren, SCA, Crawler, 3 Point Hitch, Lights, W/ W/O Front Grill Guard, NIB $200
☐ 430, 1989, Trumm, Plastic, Tractor, "Plow City 1988," Green, NIB $45
☐ 720, 1995, Yoder, Plastic, Tractor, Industrial Standard With Pony Start Or Electric Start, NIB $70
☐ 820, 1983, Trumm, CA, WFE, Custom, NIB $65
☐ 820, 1992, Trumm, CA, WFE, Small Front Wheels, Clam Shell Fenders, NIB $75
☐ 2010, 2003, Ertl/RC, Die, Crawler, "23rd Annual Plow City 2003," FB-2630, NA
☐ 2010, 2003, Ertl/RC, Die, Industrial Crawler, Blade and Ripper, "Collector Edition," 15472A, NA
☐ 2010, 2004, Ertl/RC, Die, Industrial, Crawler, TBE15634, NA
☐ 2010, 2004, Ertl/RC, Die, Crawler, Without Blade, Green, No. 15482, NA
☐ 4230, 1978, Sigomec, Die, Tractor, Fenders, No Cab, Yellow Industrial 2600, Recast With Loader in 1990, Excellent-NIB $65-90
☐ 4430, 1990, Sigomec, Die, Tractor, No Cab, With Loader, Yellow Industrial 200, NIB $90
☐ 4430, 1985, Sigomec, Die, Tractor, Argentina, WFE, 450, NIB $90

1/25 Scale Indus. & Crawlers:

☐ Excavator, 1997, Model Crafters, Wood, Model 20LC, Hydraulic, NA

1/32 Scale Indus. & Crawlers:

☐ Utility/Loader, 1991, Ertl, Die, 5647DO, NA
☐ Utility/Loader, 1991, Ertl, Die, With Attachments, 5648EF, NA
☐ Wagon, 1985, Sigomec, Barge, Industrial Yellow, Rear Hitch, Decal Rear Endgate, 512, NA

1/43 Scale Indus. & Crawlers:

☐ LI, 1995, SpecCast, Die, Industrial Tractor, JDM0681, NIB $15
☐ MT, 1995, SpecCast, Pewter, Crawler, JDMO62, NIB $18
☐ 450C, 1993, SpecCast, Pewter, Crawler, JDM023, NIB $18
☐ 1010, 1996, Hartz-P, Pewter, Crawler, With Blade, JDM084, NIB $28
☐ 3185, 1984, NPS, PI, Tractor, Yellow Or Green, NIB $15

1/50 Scale Indus. & Crawlers:

☐ Crawler, 2004, Ertl/RC, Die, 650H, TBE15631, NA

☐ Excavator, 690, 1997, Ertl, Die, 5260EO, NIB $25
☐ Excavator, 690, 1992, LW, Pewter, W/ W/O Serial No, NIB $30
☐ Log Skidder, 2004, Ertl/RC, Die, 648G III Log Skidder, TBE15662, NA
☐ Wheel Loader, 2004, Ertl/RC, Die, 824J, TBE15633, NA

1/64 Scale Indus. & Crawlers:

☐ Backhoe-Loader, 1983, Ertl, Die, WFE, Part of "Mighty Mover" Series, 573, NIP $6
☐ Bulldozer, 1995, Ertl, Die, 566, New Color and Decals, NIP $7
☐ 40, 1989, Messer, SC, Crawler, Green With Black Or Yellow Tracks, Custom, NIP $12
☐ 430, 1989, Messer, SC, Crawler, Green With Yellow Stripe, Custom, NIP $12
☐ 430, 2000, Ertl, Die, "20th Annual Plow City Show," Gold, NIP $20
☐ 700A, 1989, Keith/Matsen, SC, Tractor, Model, WFE, Custom, NIP $30
☐ 730, 1988, Keith, SC, Tractor, NF Or WFE, Custom, NIP $35
☐ 830, 1988, Keith, SC, 830 Model, WFE, Custom, NIP $35
☐ LA, 1988, CC, SC, WFE, With or Without Mower, Industrial Yellow, Custom, NIP $40
ALSO SAME, Except For *Model Farming* Magazine, Custom, NA

1/128 Scale Indus & Crawlers:

☐ Wagon, 1990, Ertl, Die, Barge, Non-Steerable, Part Of "Micro" Tractor Set, 2572FO, NA
☐ Crawler, 1990, Micro Machines, Die, 50 Series, WFE, Cab, Crude, NA

1/160 Scale Indus & Crawlers:

☐ Backhoe/Loader, 1997, GHQ, Pewter, 310A, Kit, 53-006, NA

Farm Sets

Organized By Scale, And Year Produced

1/16 Scale Farm Sets:

☐ 1964, Ertl, Die, 3020, Disc, Plow, Flare Box Wagon In Flat Boy Box, 536, NIB $950
☐ 1964, Ertl, Die, 3020 Flare Box Wagon In Flat Box, 537, NIB $800
☐ 1966, Ertl, Die, 3020 Flare Box Wagon In Bubble Box, 537, NIB $400
☐ 1974, Ertl, Die, 7520 W/Yellow Frame, Fold Over Disc, 586, NIB $700
☐ 1974, Ertl, Die, 2010 Peak Hood W/Barge Wagon, 587, NIB $45
☐ 1979, Ertl, Die, 4440 W/Skid Loader & Barge Wagon, Shed Box, 502, NIB $140
☐ 1987, ScaMo, Offset Transport, Part of Deluxe 4-Piece Farm Set, 915 Or 315 Disc Set, NIB $30

□ 1990, ScaMo, Die, 4020, W/Barn, Disc, Plow, And Wagon, NIB $30
□ 1990, Ertl, Die, Size Combination, 1/16 & 1/43 Scale Unstyled A Tractors, NIB $30
□ 1994, Ertl, Die, 70 With Hay Rake, 4166AO, NIB $30
□ 1994, Ertl, Die, 630 LP, With Wagon, 5759EO, NIB $25
□ 1994, Riecke, Custom, Styled B, Green Running Gear & Wooden Hay Rack, NA
□ 1995, Ertl, Die, 630 W/Flare Box Wagon, 5759, NIB $25
□ 1997, Ertl, Die, BR Tractor And Wagon Set, TBE5761, NIB $30
□ 1997, Ertl, Die, B Tractor, Wagon And Corn Load, Foxfire Driver, NIB $40
□ 2000, Ertl, Die, Baler Mover Set, TBE15041, NA
□ 2002, Ertl/RC, Die, 50/60 Series, 50th Anniversary Collector, TBE15344A, NA
□ 2002, Ertl/RC, Die, 50 and 60 Series, 1/16, "50th Anniversary Collector Set," TBE15344, NA
□ 2003, Ertl/RC, Die, 6410 Industrial Tractor/Mower, TBE15504, NA
□ 2003, Ertl/RC, Die, Tractor and Implement Set, TBEK37008, NA
□ 2003, Ertl/RC, Die, Construction Assortment, TBEK37O14, NA
□ Ertl, Die, 3020 & Disc, Planter, Wagon, NIB $495

1/32 Scale Farm Sets:

□ 1976, Ertl, Die, Farm To Market Set: Dealer Truck, Wagon, Tractor, 5504DO, NA
□ 1995, Siku, Die, 3300 & Wagon, NIB $25
□ 1996, Siku, Die, 3400 W/Irrigation Equipment, Wagon, NIB $40
□ 1996, Ertl, Die, JD Dealership Ford Pickup, Trailer & Skid Steer Loader, 5923, NIB $33
□ 2001, Ertl/RC, Die, Tractor And Barge Wagon, Reintroduction (of 1979 Set), TBE70, NA
□ 2003, Ertl/RC, Die, 17-Piece Value Set/Tractor, Plow, Wagon And Accessories, TBE15474, NA
□ 2003, Ertl/RC, Die, Construction Assortment, TBEK37011, NA
□ 2003, Siku, Die, 6820S And Lanz Bulldog Silver Set, "10 Years Modellbrose Friedburg Show," Tyrol Toys, NA
□ 2004, Cursor, Die, 5620-5720-5820 Series, With Loader, Serial-Numbered, Limited Edition, "John Deere Werke Mannheim 2003," NA
□ Set, 2004, Siku, Die, 6620 Tractor And Seed Drill, NA
□ Set, 2004, Britains/RC, Plastic, Tractor & Barn, 34850, NA
□ Set, 2004, Britains/RC, Plastic, Gator, Trailer and Lawn Shed, 34851, NA
□ Set, 2004, Britains/RC, Plastic, Backhoe/Loader, 34849, NA
□ Set, 2004, Britains/RC, Plastic, Wheeled Loader & Dump, 34852, NA
□ Set, 2004, Britains/RC, F, Combine & Gravity Wagon, 34853, NA
□ Set, 2004, Britains/RC, F, Tractor, Wagon & Garden Tractor, 34854, NA

1/43 Scale Farm Sets:

□ 1990, Ertl, Die, Unstyled A 1/43 & 1/16 Scale, Steel Wheels, 5532CO, NIB $35
□ 1995, SpecCast, Pewter, MT, MC Crawler 2010, 4955, 110 Waterloo Boy 4020, NIB $60

1/50 Scale Farm Sets:

□ 2002, Ertl/RC, Die, Construction Assortment, TBE2342, NA
□ 2003, Ertl/RC, Die, Construction Assortment, TBEK37O13, NA

1/64 Scale Farm Sets:

□ 1960, Ertl, Die, Historical Set, 7 Tractors On Vertical Gold Card, NIP $175
□ 1961, Ertl, D, Historical Set, Carton, 7 Boxed Tractors W/Hooks, 560, NIP $70
□ 1972, Ertl, Die, Same As 1961 Set, But 8 Boxed Tractors, W/Hooks, NIP $60
□ 1974, Ertl, Die, Historical Set, 8 Pieces In Shadow Box, 1375, NIP $225
□ 1974, Ertl, Die, Historical Set, 8 Pc, Card, Same As Shadow Box Set, 1370 0, NIP $150
□ 1974, Ertl, Die, On Card Instead Of Box, NIP $100
□ 1985, Ertl, Die, Historical Set Of 8 Pieces No Hooks, 593, NIP $50
□ 1989, Ertl, Die, Historical Set, 4 Pieces, Waterloo Boy, G, M, R, More Detail On R Rubber Tires, Bubble Pack, 5523EO, NIP $12
□ 1989, Ertl, Die, Four Piece Grain Set: Grain Truck, Grain Auger, Gravity Feed Wagon, Tractor, 5566DO, NIP $30
□ 1989, Ertl, Die, Four Piece Fertilizer Set: Fertilizer Truck, Plow, Spreader, Tractor, 5567DO, NIP $30
□ 1994 Ertl, Die, Skid Steer Loader, Construction Truck, NIP $12
□ 1994, Ertl, D, Dubuque Tractor Set, 3305, 430T, 430S, 5726, NIP $25
□ 1994, Ertl, Die, 4WD Tractor, Planter, Mulch Tiller, NIP $20
□ 1995, Ertl, Die, Tractor, Mower-Conditioner, Rake, Baler, Bale Throw Wagon, 5626, NIP $20
□ 1995, Ertl, Die, 7800 Square Baler, Bale Wagon, Mower, Conditioner, Hay Rake, 5626DR, NIP $20
□ 1995, Ertl, D, Dubuque #2, 330U, 430T, 430U, 5735EO, NIP $25
□ 1995, Ertl, D, Dubuque #3, 3001, 4301, & 430C, 5736EO, NIP $25
□ 1995, Ertl, Die, Dubuque #4, 3330SS, 43OH, And 430V, NIP $25
□ 1995, Ertl, Die, 3 Piece Construction Set, 5841EO, NIP $18
□ 1995, Ertl, D, Skidder, Crawler, Hydraulic Excavator, 5841, NIP $22
□ 1995, Ertl, D, Log Skidder, Tractor Loader, Excavator, 2350EO, NIP $20
□ 1995, Ertl, Die, Dealer Truck With Tractor, 5933, NIP $12
□ 1996, Ertl, D, GMC Pickup/JD Tractor On Trailer, 5924, NIP $7
□ 1997, Ertl, Die, Historical Set: Overtime, M, G, 80, D, 4882AO, NIP $15
□ 1997, Ertl, Die, 4-Piece Historical Set: Overtime, JD M, JD G, 80, 4882AO, NIP $12
□ 1997, Ertl, Die, Construction Hauling Set/Backhoe-Loader, Revised, PM5574, NIP $25
□ 1997, Ertl, Die, Kenworth Semi/Drop-Deck Trailer, 2 JD, NIP $22
□ 1997, Ertl, Die, Dealership Pickup/Trailer, JD D, 4831AO, NIP $10
□ 1998, Ertl, Die, 1960 Mack B-61 Semi/Flatbed Trailer, JD 5020 Tractors, 5934EO, NIP $15
□ 1998, Ertl, Die, 1960 Mack B-61 Semi/Flatbed Trailer, JD 5020 Tractors, 5934EO, NIP $15
□ 1998, SpecCast, Die, Freightliner Semi W/7000 Series Tractors' Van, 34016, NIP $18
□ 1998, SpecCast, Die, Freightliner Semi W/7000 Series Tractors' Van, 34016, NIP $18
□ 1999, Ertl, Die, 60 Series Historical Set: 60 RC, 620 Wheatland, 620WF, 5862EO, 4301 Crawlers, Natl Toy Truck 'N Construction Show, NIP $45
□ 2000, ED, F-350 Dealer Flatbed, W/8410 tractor, TBE5799, NIP $13
□ 2000, Ertl, D, No 2, Wagons: Auger, Hay, Flare, Bale,

& Implement Trailer & Hydro-Push Spreader, TBE36233, NA

□ 2000, Ertl, Die, Historical Set with 12 John Deere, IH, Agco, 36094, NA

□ 2000, Ertl, Die, Tractor & Implement Assortment of John Deere & Case/IH, 4445AP, NA

□ 2000, Ertl, Die, Historical Set, 10 Pieces, JD 8400T, JD Waterloo Boy, JD 5020, Case/IH Magnum, Case L, Farmall M, Hart-Parr, Ford 5000, Fordson F, Allis-Chalmers WD-45, Millenium, 12031A, NA

□ 2001, Ertl/RC, Die, Four Pieces, 4000 Series, Vintage 4010, 4020, 4320, 4620, 15216, NIP $16

□ 2002, Ertl/RC, Die, 6220 With 1590 Grain Drill Set, TBE15555, NA

□ 2002, Ertl/RC, Die, 75-Piece Die-Cast Value Set, TBE15456, NA

□ 2002, Ertl/RC, Die, 40-Piece Die-Cast Value Set, TBE 15439, NA

□ 2002, Ertl/RC, Die, Construction Assortment, TBE36310, NA

□ 2003, Ertl/RC, Die, 4430/4440/4450 3-Piece Tractor, TBE15492, NA

□ 2003, Ertl/RC, Die, 4020 Stacker Set/3 4020s, TBE15522, NA

□ 2003, Ertl/RC, Die, 40-Piece Value Set, TBEK37009, NA

□ 2003, Ertl/RC, Die, Vintage Tractor And Implement Assortment, TBEK37O16, NA

□ 2003, Ertl/RC, Die, Pickup or Tractor/Trailer Assortment, TBEK37O12, NA

□ 2003, Ertl/RC, Die, Modern Tractor and Implement Assortment, TBEK37O15, NA

□ 2003, Ertl/RC, Die, Classic Collection: 4010 And 5010, Hamilton Authenticated, NA

□ 2004, Ertl/RC, Die, 10-piece Historical Set: Waterloo Boy, Unstyled D, Styled B, 730, 4020, 4430, 4450, 8400 & 9520, 200th Anniversary, TBE15589A, NA

□ 2004, Ertl/RC, Die, 4240 Tractor With Cab & 535 Round Baler, TBE15620, NA

□ 2004, Ertl/RC, Die, 80/820/830, T6E15615, NA

□ 2004, Ertl/RC, Die, D, A, B, G, H, M, R, TBE15590, NA

□ 2004, Ertl/RC, Die, 3-Piece 4020 Stacker Set (Includes a Gold-Plated 4020 Tractor), TBE15522, NA

□ 2002, Ertl/RC, Die, 7520 4-Wheel-Drive With Disc Set, TBE5220, NA

□ Set, 2 Pieces, Die, D and 630 LP, NIP $9

□ Set, 4WD Tractor, Planter, Mulch Tiller, 5805, NIP $15

□ Set, 3 Pieces, Tractor, Planter, Disc, 544, NIP $15

□ Set, 4 Pieces, Ertl, Die, Boxed, Mistake On Printing, 5523, NIP $20

□ Set, Five Pieces, Tractor, Mower, Conditioner, Hay Rake, Baler, And Bale Throw Wagon, 5626, NIP $25

□ Set, Two Pieces, Waterloo Works, Waterloo Boy & 9400T Tractor, 15335, NIP $35

□ Set, 7 Pieces, ED, Yellow Blister Pack, No 730 Decal, 568, NIP $275

1/87 Scale Farm Sets:

□ 1981, Woodlands, Metal, Kit, Tractor Pit Stop Set: 60, Fuel Stands, Man, Trees, M112, NA

□ 2000, Ertl, Die, Semi W/Flat Trailer & 2-8310s TBE15066, NIP $15

Miscellaneous Farm Sets:

□ 2002, Ertl/RC, Building Series, Tractor with Barn, 275 Pieces, TBEK34850, NA

□ 2002, Ertl/RC, Building Series, Combine With Gravity Wagon, 600 Pieces, TBFK34853, NA

□ 2002, Ertl/RC, Building Series, Gator With Trailer And Garden Shed, 275 Pieces, TBEK34851, NA

□ 2002, Ertl/RC, Building Series, Modern Tractor With Wagon and Lawn Tractor, 600 Pieces, TBEK34854, NA

□ 2002, Ertl/RC, Building Series, Backhoe with Loader, 275 Pieces, TBEK34849, NA

□ 2002, Ertl/RC, Building Series, Wheel Loader and Dump Truck, 600 Pieces, TBEK34852, NA

□ 2002, Ertl/RC, Plastic, Implements, 3", TBEK5446, NA

□ 2004, Ertl/RC, Plastic, "Full Throttle" Construction Assortment/Tractor, Dozer & Excavator, 3", TBEK37155, NA

□ 2004, Ertl/RC, Plastic, "Full Throttle" Ag. Assortment/Tractors & Combine, 3", TBEK37154

□ 2004, Ertl/RC, Plastic, "Full Throttle" Tractor, Lights & Sound, 9", TBEK37213, NA

□ 2004, Ertl/RC, Plastic, 3" Plastic Vehicle Assortment/Gator & Tractor, TBEK36654, NA

□ 2004, Ertl/RC, Plastic, 9" Plastic Vehicle Assortment/Skid-Steer Loader, Articulated Dump Truck & Tractor/Loader, TBEK36657, NA

□ 2004, Ertl/RC, Plastic, 100-piece AG Building Block Set, Crawler & Tractor, TBEK37186, NA

□ 2004, Ertl/RC, Plastic, 50-piece AG Building Block Set/Tractors, Plastic, TBEK37185, NA

□ 2004, Ertl/RC, Plastic, Junior Pedal Tractor/Wagon, TBEK35046, NA

Pickups, Trucks, Semis

Pickups

Organized by year.

□ Pickup, 1982, Ertl, SS, Chevrolet Blazer, Dealer Pickup, 3827, 1/25 Scale, NIB $20

□ Pickup, 1984, Ertl, SS, GMC Dealer Pickup, Individual Dealer Logos Available, Sunroof, "Nothing Runs Like A Deer," Various Decals, 543DO Or 5531, 1/16 Scale, NIB $17

□ Pickup, 1991, Ertl, SS, GMC Dealer Pickup, Sun Roof, John Deere Logo On Rear Sides, 5683, NIB $17

□ Pickup, Ford Dealer Pickup, 1992, Ertl, Die, Four-Wheel Drive, 5612, 1/64 Scale, NIB $4

□ Pickup, 1992, Ertl, Die,Ford Pickup/Livestock Trailer, Four-Wheel-Drive With Tandem Axle Livestock Trailer, 5712, 1/64 Scale, NIB $8

□ Pickup, 1992, Ertl, Die,Ford Pickup/Machine Trailer, Four Wheel Drive With Tandem Axle Machine Trailer, 5619, 1/64 Scale, NIB $8

□ Pickup, 1992, Ertl, Die, GMC Pickup, "Customer Driven" Logo, Nashville Parts Expo, 5708GA, 1/64 Scale, NIB $6

□ Pickup, 1992, Ertl, Die, 1955 Chevy Cameo Bank, NIB $12

□ Pickup, 2000, Ertl, Die, Ford Service Pickup, John Deere, TBE15091

□ Pickup, 2001, 1957 Chevy With Snowblower & Shovel, 1/25 Scale, 73078, NIB $28

□ Pickup, 2001, Ertl/RC, Die, 1950 Chevy, Prestige, 15236, NIB $23

□ Pickup, 2001, SpecCast, 1957 Chevy Cameo, John Deere, 78034, NIB $28

□ Pickup, 2002, SpecCast, Die, 1932 Ford Pickup "John Deere," 1/25, 26030, NA

□ Pickup, 2002, SpecCast, Die, 1957 Ford Pickup "John Deere", With Semi, 2002, SpecCast, Die, Kenworth With "John Deere" Drop-Deck Trailer, 1/64, 30508, NA

□ Pickup, 2003, SpecCast, Die, 1937 Ford, "John Deere," 1/25, 16090, NA

□ Pickup, 2003, SpecCast, Die, 1957 Chevy And JD 110

□ Pickup, 2004, Hamilton Authenticated, Die, "John Deere" Pedal Tractor & Accessories, 1/25, NA

□ Pickup, 2004, Hamilton Authenticated, Die, 1947 Dodge, "John Deere", Seed Bag Load, 1/25, NA

□ Pickup, 2004, Ertl/RC, Die, 1938 American Bantam,

"John Deere," 1/27, TBE15628, NA
☐ Pickup, 2004, SpecCast, Die, John Deere 140 Lawn & Garden Tractor, 1/25, 78090, NA

TRUCKS:

Organized by year manufactured.

☐ Truck, 1982, Ertl, Die, Mack Bulldog Bank, Antique Mack Van Truck, 101 On Sides, Bank, 531EO, 1/25 Scale, NIB $50
☐ Truck, 1987, Ertl, Die,International Fertilizer Truck, Tandem Axle Straight Fertilizer Spreader Truck, 5544EO, 1/64 Scale, NIB $7
☐ Truck, 1987, Ertl, Die,International Milk Truck, Tandem Axle Straight Milk Truck, 5545EO, 1/64 Scale, NIB $6
☐ Truck, 1991, Ertl, Die,1030 Hawkeye Truck Bank, Dodge Stake Truck With Crate Load, #104 On Hood Side, Bank, 5687, 1/25 Scale, NIB $15
☐ Truck, 1990, Spec-Cast, Pewter, Ford Model T, Panel Delivery Truck, "Nashville Logo, CUST-103, 1/43 Scale, NIB $15
☐ Truck, 1991, Spec-Cast, Pewter, Ford Model T, Panel Delivery, NIB $15
☐ Truck, 1992, Ertl, Die,1926 Seagrave Fire Truck Bank, Fire Truck Bank, 5710EO, 1/25 Scale, NIB $18
☐ Truck, 1992, Ertl, Die, Mack Bulldog Bank, Antique Mack Van Truck, "John Deere Customer Driven--Outside Parts Sales--Nashville 1992," Bank, 5564 (Serial No.) 1/25 Scale, NIB $35
☐ Truck, 1993, Spec-Cast, Pewter, Antique Tank "1993 Nashville Aftermarket Conference And Parts Expo--Valdspar Moline Paint Co," Cust210, 1/43 Scale, NIB $20
☐ Truck, 1993, Murphy, Die, Antique Tanker Truck, "Hy-Grade Oil," PMOT-193, 1/25 Scale, NIB $15
☐ Truck, 2000, Ertl, Die, Flatbed, Ford F-350 Dealer Flatbed With JD 8410, TBE5799, NA
☐ Truck, 2000, Ertl, Die, Ford F-350 Dealer Flatbed With JD 8410, TBE5799, NA
☐ Truck, 2001, Ertl/RC, Delivery, Steel, Structor, John Deere 4440 Graphics, 15291. NIB $15
☐ Truck, 2001, SpecCast, 1957 Chevy Stakebed, John Deere, With John Deere 110 Tractor With Mower, 78018, Die, NIB $28
☐ Truck, 2001, SpecCast, 1957 Chevy Stakebed, John Deere, With John Deere 110 Tractor With Mower, 78018, Die, NIB $28
☐ Truck, 2002, Ertl/RC, Dodge Power Wagon "John Deere," NS
☐ Truck, 2002, Ertl/RC, Die, 400D Articulated Dump
☐ Truck, 2003, Ertl/RC, Die, 1947 DODGE Canopy Delivery Prestige, "John Deere," 1/25, TBE15500, NA
☐ Truck, 2004, Die-Cast Pro, 1941 Chevy Flatbed, John Deere Green, 1/16, NA
☐ Truck, Ertl, Die, Dealer Delivery494, Excellent-NIB $85-150
☐ Truck, Iowa 150th Truck With 4010 Tractor On Back, NIB $20
☐ Truck, "John Deere Parts Express," CUST-103, 1/43 Scale, NIB $15
☐ Truck, 1/50 Scale, TBE15386, NS

SEMIS:

Organized by year manufactured. Various sizes.

☐ Semi, 1982, Ertl, SS,Chevrolet Titan Parts Express, Semi-Tractor With Van Trailer, Varieties, 3124 Or 5533, 1/25 Scale, NIB $30
☐ Semi, 1985, Ertl, Die, Mack Equipment Hauler, Semi-Tractor With Drop Deck Trailer And Two Tractors With Or Without Front Weights, 5502EO, 1/64 Scale, NIB $35
☐ Semi, 1987, Ertl, Die,International Parts Express, Navistar Semi-Tractor With Van Trailer, 5535EO, 1/64 Scale, NIB $12
☐ Semi,1987, Ertl, Die, International Equipment Hauler, Tandem Axle Straight Truck With Flat Bed, 5542EO, 1/64 Scale, NIB $6
☐ Semi, 1989, Ertl, Die,Kenworth Equipment Hauler, Kenworth Semi-Tractor Wit Drop Deck Trailer And Two Tractors W/ Front Weights, 5535EO, 1/64 Scale, NIB $18
☐ Semi, 1989, Ertl, Die,Kenworth Parts Express, Kenworth Semi-Tractor With Van Trailers, T-600A Truck, 5535EO, 1/64 Scale, NIB $12
☐ Semi, 1989, Ertl, Die,Kenworth Equipment Hauler, Kenworth Semi-Tractor With Low Bed Trailer And JD Backhoe, 5574EO, 1/64 Scale, NIB $18
☐ Semi, 1989,International S Equipment Hauler, Semi-Tractor With Drop Deck Trailer And JD Backhoe In 1/32 Scale, 1/25 Otherwise, NIB $28
☐ Semi, 1991, Ertl, Die,International Equipment Hauler, Navistar Semi-Tractor With Drop Deck Trailer And Two Tractors With Front Weights, Semi Has Wide Logo Stripe, 5530EO, 1/64 Scale, NIB $18
☐ Semi, 1991, Ertl, Die,Kenworth Equipment Hauler, Kenworth Semi-Tractor With Drop Deck Trailer And JD 690C Excavator, "National Toy Truck 'N Construction Show & Midwest Specialized Transportation, Inc," 9715, 1/64 Scale, NIB $40
☐ Semi, 1992, Ertl, Die,Kenworth Parts Express, Kenworth Semi-Tractor With White Van Trailer, 5714EO, 1/64 Scale, NIB $12
☐ Semi, 1993, Ertl, Die,Kenworth Parts Express, Kenworth Semi With Van Trailer, "John Deere Parts Express--Strongbox," 5714EO, 1/64 Scale, NIB $12
☐ Semi, 1992, 1950 Chevrolet Semi, With Van Trailer, "Turbo Tiger" On Front Side Of Van, "Minneapolis--East Moline" On Top Rear Side, Parts Express, Bank, 1/43 Scale, NIB $25
☐ Semi, 1992, Promotex,Peterbilt Parts Express, Plastic, "John Deere Parts Express--Strong Box," 1/87 Scale, NIB $12
☐ Semi, 1992, Ertl, SS, International S Log Truck, Semi Tractor With Log Trailer, Vars., 1/25 Scale, 3180, NIB $30
☐ Semi, 2000, Ertl/RC, Die, With Peterbilt Vintage John Deere Van Trailer, 5456CO, NIB $22
☐ Semi, 2000, Ertl/RC, Die, With Flat Trailer And Two 8310 Tractors, TBE15066, NIB $18
☐ Semi, 2001, SpecCast, Die, Peterbilt 387 Semi, John Deere Ideal Condltlons, Van Trailer, 33505, NIB $28
☐ Semi, 2000, Ertl, Die, Parts Semi, 15023, NIB $12
☐ Semi, 2000, Ertl/RC, Die, With John Deere Van Trailer, 5457CO, NA
☐ Semi, 2001, SpecCast, Die, Peterbilt 387 Semi, John Deere Ideal Conditions, Van Trailer, 33505, NIB $18
☐ Semi, 2001, SpecCast, Die, Kenworth T-600B, Van Trailer W/John Deere Tires and Tracks, 30504, NIB $28
☐ Semi, 2001, SpecCast, 379 Semi With John Deere Driving Force, Die, Featherlite Van Trlr, 32822, NIB $28
☐ Semi, 2001, SpecCast, Die, Kenworth T-600B, Van Trailer W/John Deere Tires And Tracks, 30504, NIB $28
☐ Semi, 2001, SpecCast, 379 Semi With J Deere Driving Force, Die, Featherlite Van Trailer, 32822, NIB $28
☐ Semi, 2002, SpecCast, Die, T-600, NIB $28
☐ Semi, 2002, SpecCast, Die, T-600 Kenworth Semi With JD Tires & Tracks Van Trailer, 80504, 1/50 Scale, NIB $28
☐ Semi Tractor, 2002, Ertl/RC, Die, "Nothing Runs Like a Deere" Van Trailer, 1/64, No. 98271, NA
☐ Semi, 2003, Hamilton Authenticated, Die, Conventional, "Deer Creek Farms" Tanker and Ford 350 Pickup And Cows, White GMC, 1/64, NA
☐ Semi, 2003, Hamilton Authenticated, Die, Cabover, "Deer Creek Farms," Livestock Trailer And 1953 Ford
☐ Pickup And Cattle, 1/64, NA
☐ Semi, 2003, Hamilton Authenticated, Die, Peterbilt 377A Semi Grain Trailer, "Deer Creek Farms," And John Deere 630 Tractor And Corn Picker, 1/64, NA
☐ Semi, 2003, Hamilton Authenticated, Die, Conventional Semi, "Nothing Runs Like A Deere," Van Trailer, 1/64, Farm Scene, NA
☐ Semi, 2003, Hamilton Authenticated, Die, Cabover,

"Nothing Runs Like A Deere," Van Trailer, 1/64, Combine Scene, NA
 Semi, 2003, Hamilton Authenticated, Die, Conventional Semi, "Nothing Runs Like A Deere," Van Trailer, 1/64, Combine Scene, NA
 Semi, 2003, Hamilton Authenticated, Die, Cabover, "Nothing Runs Like A Deere," Van Trailer, 1/64, Farm Scene, NA
 Semi, 2003, SpecCast, Die, "John Deere - Reshaping Boundries," Van Trailer, 1/64, 36519, NA
 Semi, 2004, Ertl/RC, Die, Kenworth Van Trailer, "John Deere STS graphics," 1/64, TBE15564, NA
 Semi, 2004, Nolt, Kenworth, Bulk Feed Delivery Tanker, 1/64, 4520, NA
 Semi, 2004, Wiking, Plastic, "John Deere Technologie," Van Trailer, 1/87, 537-03-42, NA
 Semi, 2004, Siku, Die, Drop Deck Trailer & 2-JOHN DEERE 6920S Tractors, 1/87, 1837, NA
 Semi, 2004, Hamilton Authenticated, Die, 1950s Van Trailer, "John Deere," 1/25, NA
 Semi, 2004, Ertl/RC, Die, GMC Cabover Vintage Semi, "200th Birthday" John Deere Van Trailer, 1/25, Prestige Series, TBE15629, NA
 Semi, Spec-Cast, Deere Des Moines, 30145, NIB $28
 Semi, Spec-Cast, John Deere "Sign Of Choice," 31029, NIB $28
 Semi, Spec-Cast, Deere Gettel & Company, 32635, NIB $28
 Semi, Spec-Cast, John Deere Lawn Tractors, 32639, NIB $28
 Semi, Spec-Cast, John Deere Tractor/Combine, 32640, NIB $28
 Semi, Spec-Cast, John Deere 160th Anniversary, 32643, NIB $32
 Semi, Spec-Cast, John Deere 9000 Series, 32644, NIB $28
 Semi, Spec-Cast, John Deere Adamstown, 32711, NIB $28
 Semi, Spec-Cast, John Deere "Tradition," 32728, NIB $28
 Semi, Spec-Cast, John Deere "Driving Force," 32822, NIB $28
 Truck, Spec-Cast, John Deere Gas Truck, 33039, NIB $28
 Semi, Spec-Cast, John Deere with Box Van, 33040, NIB $28
 Semi, Spec-Cast, John Deere "Tires & Tracks," 33504, NIB $28
 Semi, Spec-Cast, John Deere w/53' Trailer "Ideal Conditions Are Such A Bore," 33505, NIB $28
 Semi, Spec-Cast, John Deere "Gator" w/53' Trailer, 33514, NIB $24
 Semi, Kenworth Semi With JD Tires And Tracks Van Trailer, 80504, 1/50 Scale, NA
 Semi, Log Hauler, 5532DO, NA

Various Other JD Items

Organized in alphabetical order.

 Airplane, 1986, Wood, Glider, "John Deere Days," 10 Inches Long, NIB $12
 Airplane, 1992, Spec-Cast, Die, John Deere Logo, 35002, 12 Inch Wingspan, NIB $75
 Antique Buildings, 1987, Cardboard Buildings, 1/16 Scale, NIB $50
 Auto, 1907 Type B Motor Car, 1992, Murphy, Die, Deere-Clark Auto, Regular, DSO-459, 1/20, NIB $25
 ALSO SAME, Except Gold Plated, NIB $75
 Auto, 1907 Type C Motor Car, 1993, Murphy, Die, Deere-Clark Auto, White Balloon Tires, "Gentleman's Roadster," "JD Customer Roundup Nashville 1993," Regular, DSO504, 1/20, NIB $25
 ALSO SAME, Except Gold, NIB $75
 Blacksmith Shop, 1990, Cardboard Blacksmith Shop, 1/16 Scale, NA
 Bank, John Deere Mechanical Bank, 1982, CI, "Bank On John Deere Quality," 10 Inches, NIB $75
 Bank, John Deere Mechanical Bank, 1985, CI, "Bank On John Deere Quality," Repro, 10 Inches, NIB $40
 Bank, Mail Box Bank/Bird, 1960s, Ertl, SS, Opening Door And Lock, Metal Flag, With Or Without Bird On Top, Two-Legged Deer Decal, 5505, Or 5589UO, 6 Inches Long, NIB $75
 Bank, Mail Box Bank, 1990, Ertl, SS, Opening Door & Lock, 5589UO, 6 Inches Long, NIB $15
 Bank, Centennial Drum Bank, 1937, Tin, Barrel Bank, "John Deere Tractors--Centennial 1837-1937," 3 1/2 Inches, NIB $150
 Bank, Torq Gard Bank, 1970s, Cardboard & Tin, Miniature Oil Can Bank, 3 inches, NIB $65
 Bicycle, 1890s Bicycle/Deer Model A, 1993, Murphy, Die, Bicycle With Deer Riding It, "JD Customer Roundup Nashville 1993," Regular Or Gold-Plated, DSO507, 4 1/4" High, NIB $15
 Circular Saw, 1982, Ertl, Die, Gray And Black, Sound And Blade Action, 5503, 8 3/8 Inches Long, 2 1/2 HP, NIB $25
 Engine, 2004, Turtle Creek, Gas Engine In Wooden Box, Custom, 1/64, NA
 Farm Display, Vindex Farm Display, 1930, Cardboard, Farm Scene With Three-Dimensional Barn And Silo, 1/16 Scale, Extremely Rare, $1000s Of Dollars
1/8 Scale Implements
 Gator, 1995, Ertl, Die, 6 X 4, 5748FO, 1/8 Scale, NIB $100
 Gator, 2001, ScaMo, Die, FY-1020, 1/8 Scale, NIB $100
 Gator, 2002, ScaMo, Die, Trail, 1/8, FY-1022, NA
 Gator, 2002, ScaMo, Die, Worksite, 1/8, FY-1023, NA
 Gator, 2002, Ertl/RC, Plastic, Foot-to-Floor, TBE 15464, NA
 Gator, 2002, Ertl/RC, Plastic, Worksite, Yellow Battery-Operated, TBE15519, NA
 Gator, 2003, Peg-Perego, Plastic, Worksite, 12-Volt, Ride-On, 2-Speed, NA
 Gator, 2004, Ertl/RC, Plastic, Power, Electronic Hoist, TBEK351O2, NA
 Railroad Box Car, 1992, Murphy, Plastic, "1912 80th Anniversary 1992--John Deere Company--Columbus, Ohio" On Brass Plate, "John Deere Plow Co.--Columbus, Ohio," 2250 Made, 599, O Gauge, NIB $100
 Railroad Flatcar, 2004, Athearn, Die, John Deere Model B Tractors, 1/87, 8150, NA
 Railroad Flatcar, 2004, Athearn, Die, Milwaukee 40' Flatcar With 2 John Deere Model B Tractors, 1/87, 8151, NA
 Railroad Flatcar, 2004, Athearn, Die, Sante Fe 40' Flatcar With 2 John Deere Model B Tractors, 1/87, 8153, NA
 Railroad Flatcar, 2004, Athearn, Die, D&RGW 40' Flatcar With 2 John Deere Model B Tractors, 1/87, 8152, NA
 Railroad Flatcar, 2004, Athearn, Die, CB&Q Flatcar With 2 Waterloo Boy Tractors, 1/87, 8155, NA
 Railroad Flatcar, 2004, Athearn, Die, CGW Flatcar With 2 Waterloo Boy Tractors, 1/87, 8156, NA
 Railroad Flatcar, 2004, Athearn, Die, Union Pacific 40 Flatcar With 2 John Deere Model 50 Tractors, 1/87, 8160, NA
 Railroad Flatcar, 2004, Athearn, Die, Burlington Northern 40' Flatcar With 2 John Deere Model 50 Tractors, 1/87, 8161, NA
 Snow Blower, 1988, Standi, Plastic, Attaches To Rear Of Tractor, NA
 Snowblower, Shovel, Gas Can, 1/25, 78038, NA
 Van, 2002, SpecCast, Die, Peterbilt Box, "John Deere," 1/64, 33040, NA
 Van, 2004, Britains/RC, Die, Transit, "John Deere," 1/32, 40882, NA
 Wagon, 1981, Roddenbury, Wood, Child's Repro, NA
 Wagon Of Early 1900s John Deere Wagon, 36 Inches Long Box, NIB $500
 Wagon, 1981, Wood, Child's Wagon, Similar To Sears Roebuck Co. Early 1900s, 42 Inches Long Box, NIB $600